١٤/٩/١٢

CPG
3|06

EBA

TOT | OSG | FRI

200 Quilt Blocks to Mix and Match

D0258920

200 Quilt Blocks to Mix and Match

Davina Thomas

David and Charles

A DAVID & CHARLES BOOK

First published in 2005 in the UK by
David & Charles
Brunel House
Newton Abbot
Devon

Copyright © 2005
Quarto Publishing plc

All rights reserved. No part of this
publication may be reproduced, stored
in a retrieval system or transmitted,
in any form or by any means –
electronic, mechanical, photocopying,
recording or otherwise – without the
prior written permission of the
copyright owner.

A catalogue record for this
book is available from the
British Library.

ISBN 0 7153 2236 2

Conceived, designed and produced by
Quarto Publishing plc
The Old Brewery
6 Blundell Street
London N7 9BH

QUAR: MMQ

Editor Michelle Pickering
Art editor Tim Pattinson
Designer Lizzie Ballantyne
Photographers Paul Forrester,
Phil Wilkins
Illustrator Kuo Kang Chen
Assistant art director Penny Cobb

Art director Moira Clinch
Publisher Paul Carslake

Colour separation by Pica Digital,
Singapore
Printed by SNP Leefung Printers
Limited, China

9 8 7 6 5 4 3 2 1

Visit our website at
www.davidandcharles.co.uk

David & Charles books are available
from all good bookshops; alternatively
you can contact our Orderline on
(0)1626 334555 or write to us at
FREEPOST EX2 110, David & Charles
Direct, Newton Abbot, TQ12 4ZZ (no
stamp required UK mainland).

Contents

BARNET LIBRARIES		
Bertrams	08.02.06	
746.46	£14.99	

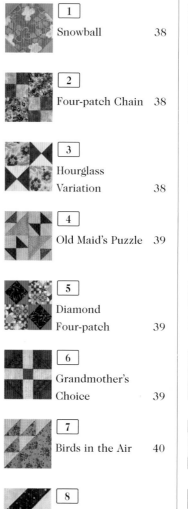

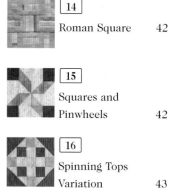

CHAPTER 3
Techniques and Templates 104

Introduction

Block 16, Spinning Tops Variation

Block 59, Carrie Nation Quilt

Block 146, Fly Foot

For hundreds of years, people (mainly women) have been sewing small pieces of fabric together to create larger ones and recycling scraps of clothing to make quilts. Developing on from this, quilters intentionally cut up larger fabrics and sewed the smaller pieces together in deliberate patterns that they found pleasing. This eventually evolved into block patchwork as we know it, usually designed on a geometric grid. Sewing pieced blocks and joining them together to make a larger item has long been a favourite technique for creating the warm, decorative and useful quilts, hangings and throws found in so many homes.

This book will inspire you to take on the challenge of creating your own quilts, transforming humble fabric pieces into unique quilts, wall hangings and accessories in a kaleidoscope of colourful contemporary and traditional designs. From simple squares and chequerboards to elaborate star blocks, discover new ways to combine colour and pattern. The 200 quilt blocks in this book – including many original designs as well as traditional block patterns – are all 6in (15cm) square, making it easy to mix and match them in any combination to produce a fabulous quilt, blanket or throw.

All of the techniques required are clearly explained with step-by-step photographs, from cutting the pieces to simple quilting. At-a-glance symbols denote the shapes and techniques used, plus the skill level required, so both new and experienced quilters can easily create beautiful finished works.

Colours and fabrics

The 200 blocks in this book were made using a palette of 100 fabrics. Details of the specific fabrics used are provided on pages 122–125, but you can of course sew the blocks using any fabric and colour combinations that you like. Traditional cotton fabrics have been used here, but you could substitute velvets and silks for a richer look.

You can use the same fabrics each time a block is repeated in your quilt, or you could try varying the fabrics in each block to make your quilt look more visually complex.In the example below, the colours gradually change from predominantly blue to magenta.

This book provides examples of blocks that can be mixed and matched together, but you can select any combination of blocks that you like for your quilt – the possibilities are virtually endless.

Mixing and matching blocks

As well as instructions for making 200 blocks, a selection of block combinations is included to inspire you when arranging blocks to make a quilt, plus some examples of finished quilt layouts. These aim to encourage you to look at block combinations with a fresh eye. For simplicity, the quilt layouts are shown using all the same fabrics each time a block is repeated, but for a visually more complex quilt you can vary the fabrics used in each block across the quilt. Although this looks more complicated, the piecing is still as simple as your choice of blocks dictates.

Use this book as a starting point to help you design and create unique quilts that will delight your friends and family and transform your home.

How to Use This Book

At the beginning of the book you will find an illustrated contents list showing you photographs of all 200 blocks. All you have to do is look through the list and find one you like.

Mix and match

The mix-and-match section takes you through the process of creating your own quilt, giving advice on choosing colours, calculating fabric quantities and combining blocks. There are also designs for making 17 quilts and cushion covers using a selection of blocks from the directory. They include large designs as well as small, quick-to-make ones.

Techniques and templates

This section contains detailed information on the equipment required and how to cut and sew the blocks, including helpful hints for improving accuracy. Different methods of joining blocks are also demonstrated, as well as ideas for quilting the finished piece. At the end of the section, you will find full-size templates for those blocks that require unusual or difficult shapes, plus a list of the actual fabrics used in the book.

Size

All the blocks in this book are the same size, 6in (15cm) square, so any block can be mixed and matched with the others at will.

Quilt layouts

Each quilt layout is accompanied by details of the finished size of the item, the materials required and how to construct the quilt, including tips for speed and suggestions for suitable bindings.

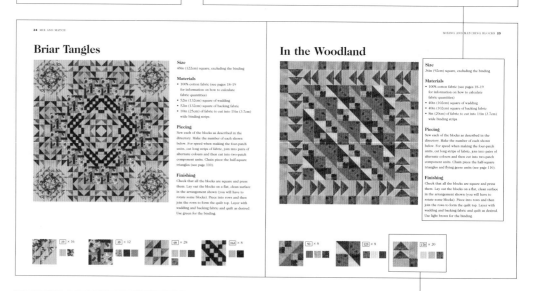

Briar Tangles

Size
48in (122cm) square, excluding the binding

Materials
• 100% cotton fabric (see pages 18–19 for information on how to calculate fabric quantities)
• 52in (132cm) square of wadding
• 52in (132cm) square of backing fabric
• 10in (25cm) of fabric to cut into 1½in (3.7cm) wide binding strips

Piecing
Sew each of the blocks as described in the directory. Make the number of each shown below. For speed when making the four-patch units, cut long strips of fabric, join into pairs of alternate colours and then cut into two-patch component units. Chain piece the half-square triangles (see page 110).

Finishing
Check that all the blocks are square and press them. Lay out the blocks on a flat, clean surface in the arrangement shown (you will have to rotate some blocks). Piece into rows and then join the rows to form the quilt top. Layer with wadding and backing fabric and quilt as desired. Use green for the binding.

In the Woodland

Size
36in (92cm) square, excluding the binding

Materials
• 100% cotton fabric (see pages 18–19 for information on how to calculate fabric quantities)
• 40in (102cm) square of wadding
• 40in (102cm) square of backing fabric
• 8in (20cm) of fabric to cut into 1½in (3.7cm) wide binding strips

Piecing
Sew each of the blocks as described in the directory. Make the number of each shown below. For speed when making the four-patch units, cut long strips of fabric, join into pairs of alternate colours and then cut into two-patch component units. Chain piece the half-square triangles and flying geese units (see page 110).

Finishing
Check that all the blocks are square and press them. Lay out the blocks on a flat, clean surface in the arrangement shown (you will have to rotate some blocks). Piece into rows and then join the rows to form the quilt top. Layer with wadding and backing fabric and quilt as desired. Use light brown for the binding.

Turning the blocks

Some of the blocks used in the quilt layouts need to be turned clockwise or anticlockwise by 90 or 180 degrees to make up the design. When assembling the blocks, check the illustration carefully and make sure the orientation of each block matches the layout.

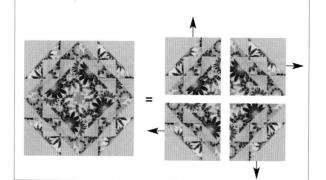

Quantity and colours

Each block used for the quilt is shown below the main illustration, accompanied by its reference number, fabric selection and how many of that block you need to make.

Block directory

The block directory contains 200 block patterns. Each one is accompanied by a photograph, fabric selection, cutting instructions, construction method, quick tips, at-a-glance symbols and ideas for matching the block with others in the directory. All of the measurements specified in the cutting instructions include a ¼in (6mm) seam allowance. Follow *either* the imperial *or* the metric measurements when cutting the pieces; never interchange between the two systems.

Understanding the symbols

Each block design is accompanied by a symbol indicating the skill level required to make it, plus symbols indicating the most difficult shapes to cut for that block and any special techniques used.

Skill level
Easy

Intermediate

Advanced

Shapes
Uses squares and rectangles only

Incorporates triangular shapes

Requires templates (provided full-size on pages 116–121)

Techniques
Involves sewing inset seams (see page 111)

Curved piecing (see page 111)

Fast piecing techniques can be used (see pages 110 and 113)

Construction guidelines

Key blocks demonstrate basic constructional techniques that are referred to throughout the directory. Step-by-step illustrations make it clear how to sew the pieces together.

Shared cutting and construction

Several blocks require the same size pieces and construction techniques, but use different fabrics and arrangements. If a block does not feature specific cutting and construction guidelines, you will find this information in the nearest previous block that does – for example, refer to block 22 for cutting and construction guidelines for making blocks 23–26.

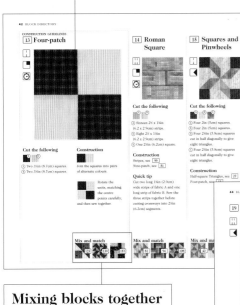

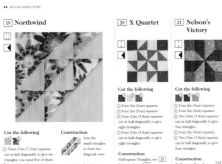

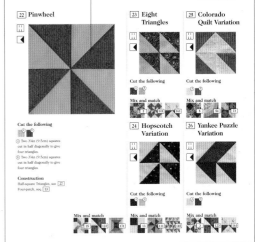

Mixing blocks together

You can use your own imagination to mix blocks or experiment with the recommendations here.

Mix and Match

This chapter will help you decide which blocks to mix and match, and features plenty of examples showing different styles to get you started. There is also guidance on the choice of colours, plus ideas on getting the most from different textile designs and how to calculate the fabric requirements for the quilt you want to make.

Colours and Fabrics

One of the most exciting features of quilts is the impact of colour. Colour can cause the greatest anxiety among quilters, with so many fabrics to choose from that it is easy to become overwhelmed. A restricted palette of 100 fabrics was used to make all 200 blocks in this book, with the fabrics being chosen to achieve a balance of plains and patterns as well as the whole spectrum of colours.

Colour theory

It is useful to learn a few basic principles of colour theory by studying a standard colour wheel. There are three primary colours on the wheel – red, yellow and blue – and these are divided by three secondary colours – orange, green and purple. The secondary colours are made by mixing the two adjacent primary colours together. The term 'value' is used to describe the lightness or darkness of a colour. Colours that are close on the colour wheel are called analogous, or harmonious; for example, yellow through to red. Colours that are opposite on the wheel are called complementary, or contrasting; for example, orange and blue. If you choose an analogous colour scheme and your fabrics are similar in value, it will look lovely but the pattern will not be as definite as it would be if you added some contrast to the colour scheme by introducing some complementary or different value colours. When choosing a complementary colour scheme, it is

Analagous colour scheme

Complementary colour scheme

Strongly contrasting colour scheme

Monochromatic colour scheme

a good idea to follow the 80:20 rule – that is, 80 per cent of one colour and 20 per cent of the complementary colour. If you use 50 per cent of each colour, they can fight and the result will not be restful to look at. Single-colour, monochromatic schemes can work very well if you use fabrics with different values and/or patterns.

Types of fabric

Cotton fabrics

The most common fabric for quilt making is 100 per cent cotton, but experienced quilters can incorporate flannels, silk, fleece or any other materials they find. Cotton fabrics are easy to work with and can be pressed to give a crisp seam. Polycottons are more springy and harder to work with and press. Always dip a small piece of the fabric into hot water to check that the colour will not run. If it does, wash it a few times before use. New, unwashed fabric has a crisp dressing that makes it easy to cut and piece, but if you have washed your fabric, you can starch it before cutting if you wish.

Textile designs

Plain or solid colours are good for breaking up busy patterns and for accentuating individual patches in a block. Striped fabrics can have many colours or just two; the designs usually run parallel to the selvage and are useful for border blocks. Large prints are harder to use than small print designs, but are useful for large centre patches. You can also cut many small patches from them in an arrangement that yields a wide variety of colours and patterns. Pictorial, or conversational, fabrics are those with pictures on. They can be cut so that a particular section is in the centre of a block, but be careful because they often have a right and wrong way up.

Try to vary the type of fabrics you use. Mix florals with geometrics and plains with pictorials. If you normally use small prints and are not confident about trying something new, you could sew some test blocks using a wider variety of patterns – combining large prints with small checks and stripes, for example. You will find that your confidence gradually increases. You can also use fabrics to make your quilt look a lot more complicated than it really is. For example, if you replace a plain square with a striped fabric, from a distance it will look as if the stripes are pieced.

Plain

Striped

Large print

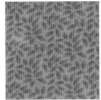

Small print

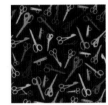

Pictorial

Floral

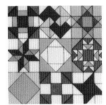

Geometric

Checked

Buying fabric

The best piece of advice is: if you like a fabric, use it. Don't agonize or worry that others may not like it; it is not their quilt. When choosing fabrics from a shop, a good tip is to find one fabric you love and then choose other fabrics to go with it. These can be similar in colour or different, depending on the effect you want to achieve. The staff can advise you and often group fabrics that they think work well together. If possible, check the fabrics in daylight by carrying them to the window; some electric lights have an orange cast that may distort the appearance of the colours.

Calculating Fabric Quantities

Unless you are making a scrap quilt from lots of different fabrics, it is important to calculate how much of each fabric you will need so that you have enough to complete the quilt. Calculating fabric quantities does require a bit of work, but it is not difficult. You just need to sit down with a clear head when you are not tired, with a piece of paper and a pencil (a calculator and fat quarter or width of fabric are useful, too, especially when using templates).

Write it down

Decide on the finished length and width of your quilt, making sure each is divisible by 6in (15cm) – remember, all the blocks in this book are 6in (15cm) square. Calculate how many blocks there will be across and down the quilt, and write this information down. Next count how many of each block there are and write that down. Make a sample of each block and decide on your fabrics. Photocopy the pages of the book with your blocks on and stick your fabrics in place. If you do not have access to a copier, trace the blocks onto freezer or greaseproof paper and stick the fabrics onto that.

Make a list of all the pieces needed for each block and their colours. Then, working colour by colour, calculate how many of each piece you need; follow the example on the opposite page if it helps make it clearer. If you have access to a quilt design program, such as Electric Quilt or Quiltpro, these can calculate the yardage for you, but be aware that they often have a fat quarter of fabric as a minimum even if you only need one small piece in the entire quilt.

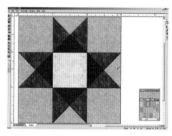

Programs such as Electric Quilt make it easy to design blocks and quilts, as well as try out different colour schemes.

Individual block design

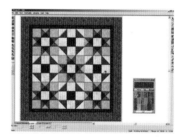

Quilt design

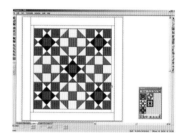

Alternative colour scheme

Fat quarters

Fabric can be purchased in ready-cut pieces called fat quarters. These are half a yard of fabric cut in half to give a quarter of a yard, but in a fat rectangle not a long thin one – that is, 20 x 18in. The metric equivalent of a fat quarter is slightly larger, at 50cm square. Fat eighths are also available; these are a fat quarter cut in half again.

Worked example: Nine-patch Blues

This quilt is 36in (90cm) square and comprises 18 of block 51 and 18 of block 136 (column A). Block 51 uses two fabrics: plain blue and patterned; block 136 uses two fabrics: white and variegated blue (column B). Find the cutting sizes for the pieces in each block. Working colour by colour, list the measurements of all the pieces of each colour for each block in column C. Multiply the figures in column C by the number of pieces required in each block and by the number of blocks (D) to give total inches or centimetres required (E). If a piece is not square, use the biggest number for your calculations; for example, for a 3½ x 2in (8.7 x 5cm) strip, multiply 3½in (8.7cm) by D. Put the width of your fabric at the top of column F; allow 40in for yardage and 20in for fat quarters (or 100cm for metreage and 50cm for fat quarters). Divide E by this figure to give the total number of strips required (F). Multiply the number of strips (F) by the width of the piece (C) to find the total fabric required. Always round up to allow for mistakes.

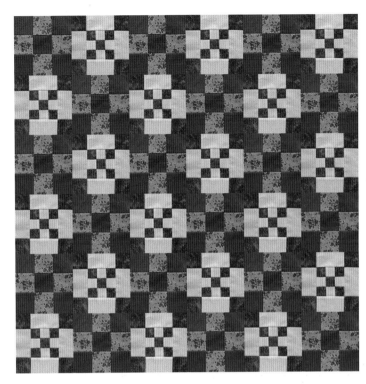

A	B	C	D	E	F
Block	Fabric	Size	Number required	Total required	40in (100cm) width
51	plain blue	2½in (6.2cm)	5 x 18	225in (558cm)	6 strips
	patterned	2½in (6.2cm)	4 x 18	180in (446.4cm)	5 strips
136	white	3½ x 2in (8.7 x 5cm)	4 x 18	252in (626.4cm)	7 strips
	white	1½in (3.7cm)	4 x 18	108in (266.4cm)	3 strips
	variegated blue	2in (5cm)	4 x 18	144in (360cm)	4 strips
	variegated blue	1½in (3.7cm)	5 x 18	135in (333cm)	4 strips

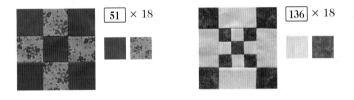

51 × 18   **136** × 18

Plain blue: 6 x 2½in (6.2cm) = 15in (38cm). The total plain blue fabric required is therefore 15in (38cm).

Patterned: 5 x 2½in (6.2cm) = 12½in (31cm). The total patterned fabric required is therefore 12½in (31cm).

White: 7 x 2in (5cm) = 14in (35cm), plus 3 x 1½in (3.7cm) = 4½in (12cm). The total white fabric required is therefore 18½in (47cm).

Variegated blue: 4 x 2in (5cm) = 8in (20cm), plus 4 x 1½in (3.7cm) = 6in (15cm). The total variegated blue fabric required is therefore 14in (35cm).

Mixing and Matching Blocks

All 200 blocks in the block directory are the same size, 6in (15cm) square, so there are thousands of possible combinations you could put together when designing your own quilt, throw or cushion. Here are a few helpful hints, but it is really a matter of personal preference.

Choosing blocks

Look through the mix-and-match examples on pages 22–35, plus the worked example on page 19. Do you prefer one style to another? For example, some have blocks with a diagonal bias that can be used to make log cabin-style arrangements or to create the effect of a block on point in the middle of your quilt. Others are more regular, with two blocks alternated. Some blocks are particularly suitable for creating the sides and corners of fake pieced borders.

Your level of sewing skills is another factor to keep in mind. All of the blocks are marked with an icon indicating the skill level required to make that block, from easy to intermediate to advanced. If you are a beginner, you may find it best to choose blocks marked with an 'easy' icon.

 Easy   Intermediate   Advanced

Fake border design, In the Woodland, page 25

These are just some of the blocks in the directory that are ideal for creating border designs for your quilt.

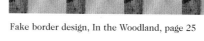

		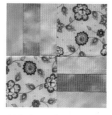		
8, Arrow	101, Long Checks	118, Around the Bend	119, Mitred Corner	138, Large Triangles and Stripes

Think also about whether you want the seam lines to meet. If you do and the first block you select is a four-patch design, try to select other four-patch blocks to combine with it. Alternately, if you combine a four-patch block with a nine-patch design, there will be less bulk at the seams and it will be less obvious if your blocks are not perfect because there are no seams to match. Another good style for this is sashed blocks, but choose two with different width sashings so that inaccurate seams will not be so obvious.

Make a sample

Always make a sample every time you sew a new block. This will enable you to check the size. The cutting measurements are rounded to the nearest ⅛in (3mm) to make them easy to see on rulers. This can mean that a block will be slightly larger or smaller than the 6in (15cm) specified. It is best to find this out at the beginning, not after you have made 20 blocks only to discover that they do not fit together. Adjust your seam allowance by the width of a thread either way to bring the blocks to the required size. See also the improving accuracy section on pages 112–113.

If you make all your sample blocks in one colour, such as blue, you will soon have a lovely collection of blocks that you can use to make a sampler quilt and all for next to no effort. Another good option for test blocks is to use Christmas fabrics, so that each year you will have a new Christmas throw to display. These test blocks can, of course, be included in the backing as a label if wished.

Testing your design

If you are not sure about some blocks, photocopy them in black and white. This will remove any colour bias that you might have and show you just the tones; you can then see if the tones balance across the quilt. You can photocopy your fabrics in black and white, too, which helps with balancing the colour values of your blocks – even if the copy shop thinks you are a bit peculiar.

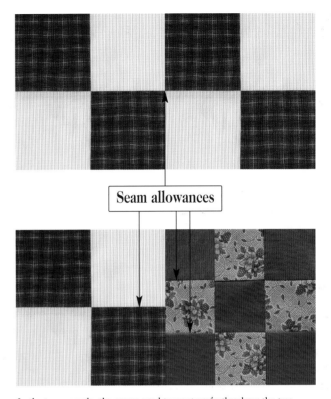

Seam allowances

In the top example, the seams need to meet perfectly where the two blocks join. There are also seam allowances from four fabrics at this meeting point on the back of the blocks, producing more bulk. In the above example, the seam allowances are spread across the seam joining the two blocks, and less-than-perfect piecing will not be as noticeable. Below, two blocks that incorporate sashings as part of their design have been joined, but the sashings are of different widths, helping to disguise any piecing inaccuracies and spread the bulk of the seam allowances.

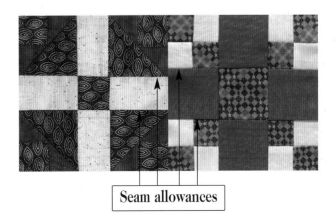

Seam allowances

Blue and Green

Size

30in (76cm) square, excluding the binding

Materials

- 100% cotton fabric (see pages 18–19 for information on how to calculate fabric quantities)
- 34in (86cm) square of wadding
- 34in (86cm) square of backing fabric
- 8in (20cm) of fabric to cut into 1½in (3.7cm) wide binding strips

Piecing

Sew each of the blocks as described in the directory. Make the number of each shown below. For speed when making the four-patch units, cut long strips of fabric, join into pairs of alternate colours and then cut into two-patch component units (see page 110).

Finishing

Check that all the blocks are square and press them. Lay out the blocks on a flat, clean surface in the arrangement shown. Piece into rows and then join the rows to form the quilt top. Layer with wadding and backing fabric and quilt as desired. Use blue or green for the binding.

  42 × 13    59 × 12

Box of Treats

Size
48in (122cm) square, excluding the binding

Materials
- 100% cotton fabric (see pages 18–19 for information on how to calculate fabric quantities)
- 52in (132cm) square of wadding
- 52in (132cm) square of backing fabric
- 10in (25cm) of fabric to cut into 1⅜in (3.7cm) wide binding strips

Piecing
Sew each of the blocks as described in the directory. Make the number of each shown below. For speed when making the four-patch units, cut long strips of fabric, join into pairs of alternate colours and then cut into two-patch component units. Chain piece the half-square triangles (see page 110).

Finishing
Check that all the blocks are square and press them. Lay out the blocks on a flat, clean surface in the arrangement shown (you will have to rotate some blocks). Piece into rows and then join the rows to form the quilt top. Layer with wadding and backing fabric and quilt as desired. Use red for the binding.

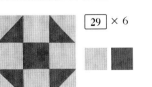 16 × 7

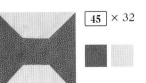 17 × 6

 29 × 6

 45 × 32

 62 × 6

 65 × 7

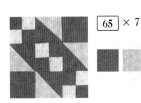

Briar Tangles

Size

48in (122cm) square, excluding the binding

Materials

- 100% cotton fabric (see pages 18–19 for information on how to calculate fabric quantities)
- 52in (132cm) square of wadding
- 52in (132cm) square of backing fabric
- 10in (25cm) of fabric to cut into 1½in (3.7cm) wide binding strips

Piecing

Sew each of the blocks as described in the directory. Make the number of each shown below. For speed when making the four-patch units, cut long strips of fabric, join into pairs of alternate colours and then cut into two-patch component units. Chain piece the half-square triangles (see page 110).

Finishing

Check that all the blocks are square and press them. Lay out the blocks on a flat, clean surface in the arrangement shown (you will have to rotate some blocks). Piece into rows and then join the rows to form the quilt top. Layer with wadding and backing fabric and quilt as desired. Use green for the binding.

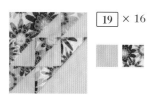 19 × 16

 35 × 12

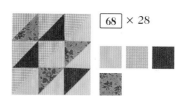 68 × 28

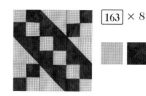 163 × 8

In the Woodland

Size

36in (92cm) square, excluding the binding

Materials

- 100% cotton fabric (see pages 18–19 for information on how to calculate fabric quantities)
- 40in (102cm) square of wadding
- 40in (102cm) square of backing fabric
- 8in (20cm) of fabric to cut into 1⅛in (3.7cm) wide binding strips

Piecing

Sew each of the blocks as described in the directory. Make the number of each shown below. For speed when making the four-patch units, cut long strips of fabric, join into pairs of alternate colours and then cut into two-patch component units. Chain piece the half-square triangles and flying geese units (see page 110).

Finishing

Check that all the blocks are square and press them. Lay out the blocks on a flat, clean surface in the arrangement shown (you will have to rotate some blocks). Piece into rows and then join the rows to form the quilt top. Layer with wadding and backing fabric and quilt as desired. Use light brown for the binding.

  93 × 8

 123 × 8

 170 × 20

Raspberry Ripple

Size

36in (92cm) square, excluding the binding

Materials

- 100% cotton fabric (see pages 18–19 for information on how to calculate fabric quantities)
- 40in (102cm) square of wadding
- 40in (102cm) square of backing fabric
- 8in (20cm) of fabric to cut into 1½in (3.7cm) wide binding strips

Piecing

Sew each of the blocks as described in the directory. Make the number of each shown below. For speed when making the four-patch units, cut long strips of fabric, join into pairs of alternate colours and then cut into two-patch component units. Chain piece the half-square triangles (see page 110).

Finishing

Check that all the blocks are square and press them. Lay out the blocks on a flat, clean surface in the arrangement shown (you will have to rotate some blocks). Piece into rows and then join the rows to form the quilt top. Layer with wadding and backing fabric and quilt as desired. Use pale pink for the binding.

  11 × 12

  81 × 12

  110 × 8

   146 × 4

Sunrise

Size

48in (122cm) square, excluding the binding

Materials

- 100% cotton fabric (see pages 18–19 for information on how to calculate fabric quantities)
- 52in (132cm) square of wadding
- 52in (132cm) square of backing fabric
- 10in (25cm) of fabric to cut into 1½in (3.7cm) wide binding strips

Piecing

Sew each of the blocks as described in the directory. Make the number of each shown below. For speed when making the four-patch units, cut long strips of fabric, join into pairs of alternate colours and then cut into two-patch component units. Chain piece the half-square triangles (see page 110).

Finishing

Check that all the blocks are square and press them. Lay out the blocks on a flat, clean surface in the arrangement shown (you will have to rotate some blocks). Piece into rows and then join the rows to form the quilt top. Layer with wadding and backing fabric and quilt as desired. Use red or orange for the binding.

 16 × 12

 17 × 24

 62 × 4

 65 × 24

Geese in the Barn

Size

36in (92cm) square, excluding the binding

Materials

- 100% cotton fabric (see pages 18–19 for information on how to calculate fabric quantities)
- 40in (102cm) square of wadding
- 40in (102cm) square of backing fabric
- 8in (20cm) of fabric to cut into 1½in (3.7cm) wide binding strips

Piecing

Sew each of the blocks as described in the directory. Make the number of each shown below. For speed, chain piece the half-square triangles (see page 110). For a scrap-quilt look, sort your fabrics into dark and light values and make the blocks using a random selection.

Finishing

Check that all the blocks are square and press them. Lay out the blocks on a flat, clean surface in the arrangement shown (you will have to rotate some blocks). Piece into rows and then join the rows to form the quilt top. Layer with wadding and backing fabric and quilt as desired. Use a dark tone for the binding or, if you have made a scrap quilt, you could piece strips for the binding, too.

114 × 4

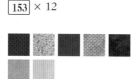
153 × 12

180 × 20

Windy Day

Size
48in (122cm) square, excluding the binding

Materials
- 100% cotton fabric (see pages 18–19 for information on how to calculate fabric quantities)
- 52in (132cm) square of wadding
- 52in (132cm) square of backing fabric
- 10in (25cm) of fabric to cut into 1⅜in (3.7cm) wide binding strips

Piecing
Sew each of the blocks as described in the directory. Make the number of each shown below. For speed, chain piece the half-square triangles (see page 110).

Finishing
Check that all the blocks are square and press them. Lay out the blocks on a flat, clean surface in the arrangement shown (you will have to rotate some blocks). Piece into rows and then join the rows to form the quilt top. Layer with wadding and backing fabric and quilt as desired. Use green for the binding.

 55 × 16

 64 × 8

 80 × 8

 124 × 24

 141 × 8

Spring Cushion

Size

18in (45cm) square

Materials

- 100% cotton fabric (see pages 18–19 for information on how to calculate fabric quantities)
- 20in (50cm) square of wadding
- 20in (50cm) square of backing fabric
- 18in (45cm) square cushion pad

Piecing

Sew each of the blocks as described in the directory. Make the number of each shown below. The cushion cover includes nine-patch, striped and flying geese units, so it is an ideal small project for brushing up your techniques.

Finishing

Check that all the blocks are square and press them. Lay out the blocks on a flat, clean surface in the arrangement shown (you will have to rotate some blocks). Piece into rows and then join the rows together. Layer with wadding and backing fabric and quilt as desired. Make a cushion back and sew right sides together with the quilted front. Turn through and insert a cushion pad.

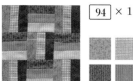 **94** × 1

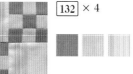 **132** × 4

 161 × 4

Summer Cushion

Size

18in (45cm) square

Materials

- 100% cotton fabric (see pages 18–19 for information on how to calculate fabric quantities)
- 20in (50cm) square of wadding
- 20in (50cm) square of backing fabric
- 18in (45cm) square cushion pad

Piecing

Sew each of the blocks as described in the directory. Make the number of each shown below.

Finishing

Check that all the blocks are square and press them. Lay out the blocks on a flat, clean surface in the arrangement shown. Piece into rows and then join the rows together. Layer with wadding and backing fabric and quilt as desired. Make a cushion back and sew right sides together with the quilted front. Turn through and insert a cushion pad.

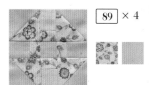 **89** × 4

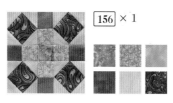 **156** × 1

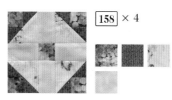 **158** × 4

Christmas Cushion

Size
18in (45cm) square

Materials
- 100% cotton fabric (see pages 18–19 for information on how to calculate fabric quantities)
- 20in (50cm) square of wadding
- 20in (50cm) square of backing fabric
- 18in (45cm) square cushion pad

Piecing
Sew each of the blocks as described in the directory. Make the number of each shown below. For speed, chain piece the quarter-square triangles and flying geese units (see page 110).

Finishing
Check that all the blocks are square and press them. Lay out the blocks on a flat, clean surface in the arrangement shown (you will have to rotate some blocks). Piece into rows and then join the rows together. Layer with wadding and backing fabric and quilt as desired. Make a cushion back and sew right sides together with the quilted front. Turn through and insert a cushion pad.

 115 × 5 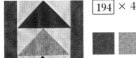 194 × 4

Crack Those Curves

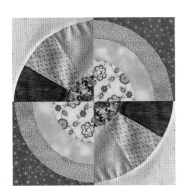

Size
12in (30cm) square

Materials
- 100% cotton fabric (see pages 18–19 for information on how to calculate fabric quantities)
- 14in (35cm) square of wadding
- 14in (35cm) square of backing fabric
- 12in (30cm) square cushion pad

Piecing
Sew each of the blocks as described in the directory. Make the number of each shown below. Cut the template pieces on both blocks larger around the sides of the cushion because this will help increase the accuracy of your blocks and also give you sufficient seam allowance to make the blocks into a cushion. This is an ideal small project for you to practise sewing curves.

Finishing
Check that all the blocks are square and press them. Lay out the blocks on a flat, clean surface in the arrangement shown (you will have to rotate some blocks). Piece into pairs and then join the pairs together. Add a border to make a larger cushion. Layer with wadding and backing fabric and quilt as desired. It would look good quilted in concentric circles. Make a cushion back and sew right sides together with the quilted front. Turn through and insert a cushion pad.

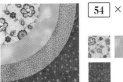 54 × 2 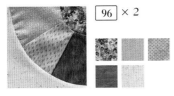 96 × 2

Star Boxes

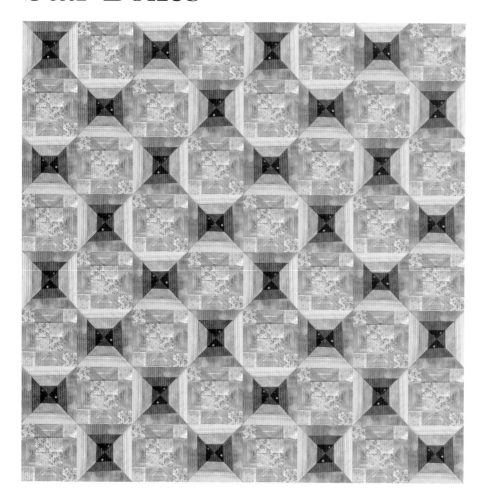

Size
48in (122cm) square, excluding the binding

Materials
- 100% cotton fabric (see pages 18–19 for information on how to calculate fabric quantities)
- 52in (132cm) square of wadding
- 52in (132cm) square of backing fabric
- 10in (25cm) of fabric to cut into 1½in (3.7cm) wide binding strips

Piecing
Sew each of the blocks as described in the directory. Make the number of each shown below.

Finishing
Check that all the blocks are square and press them. Lay out the blocks on a flat, clean surface in the arrangement shown (you will have to rotate some blocks). Piece into rows and then join the rows to form the quilt top. Layer with wadding and backing fabric and quilt as desired. Use pink for the binding.

 103 × 32

 171 × 32

Passion for Purple

Size

48in (122cm) square, excluding the binding

Materials

- 100% cotton fabric (see pages 18–19 for information on how to calculate fabric quantities)
- 52in (132cm) square of wadding
- 52in (132cm) square of backing fabric
- 10in (25cm) of fabric to cut into 1½in (3.7cm) wide binding strips

Piecing

Sew each of the blocks as described in the directory. Make the number of each shown below. For speed when making the four-patch units, cut long strips of fabric, join into pairs of alternate colours and then cut into two-patch component units. Chain piece the half-square triangles (see page 110).

Finishing

Check that all the blocks are square and press them. Lay out the blocks on a flat, clean surface in the arrangement shown. Piece into rows and then join the rows to form the quilt top. Layer with wadding and backing fabric and quilt as desired. Use purple for the binding.

  56 × 32

 188 × 32

Sashed Surprise

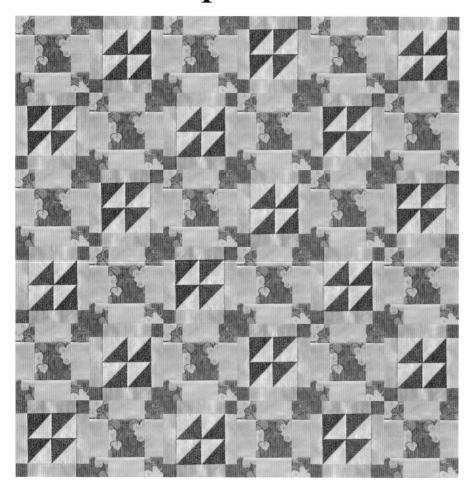

Size

36in (92cm) square, excluding the binding

Materials

- 100% cotton fabric (see pages 18–19 for information on how to calculate fabric quantities)
- 40in (102cm) square of wadding
- 40in (102cm) square of backing fabric
- 8in (20cm) of fabric to cut into 1½in (3.7cm) wide binding strips

Piecing

Sew each of the blocks as described in the directory. Make the number of each shown below. For speed when making the nine-patch units, cut long strips of fabric, join into sets of three and then cut into three-patch component units. Chain piece the half-square triangles (see page 110).

Finishing

Check that all the blocks are square and press them. Lay out the blocks on a flat, clean surface in the arrangement shown (you will have to rotate some blocks). Piece into rows and then join the rows to form the quilt top. Layer with wadding and backing fabric and quilt as desired. Use green or pink for the binding.

 182 × 18

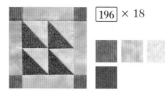 196 × 18

Star Sampler

Size
48 x 36in (122 x 92cm), excluding the binding

Materials
- 100% cotton fabric (see pages 18–19 for information on how to calculate fabric quantities)
- 52 x 40in (132 x 102cm) of wadding
- 52 x 40in (132 x 102cm) of backing fabric
- 10in (25cm) of fabric to cut into 1½in (3.7cm) wide binding strips

Piecing
Choose your favourite star blocks from throughout the directory; in this example there are not more than four blocks of any one design. You need 48 blocks in total. Either make them as shown here in a wild explosion of colour or choose your colours more carefully to tone together.

Finishing
Check that all the blocks are square and press them. Lay out the blocks on a flat, clean surface in the arrangement shown. Piece into rows and then join the rows to form the quilt top. Layer with wadding and backing fabric and quilt as desired. Use a toning colour for the binding.

| 15 | 21 | 37 | 40 | 61 | 74 | 108 | 152 | 169 | 186 | × 1 |

| 17 | 18 | 47 | 48 | 67 | 95 | 109 | 115 | 177 | × 2 |

| 103 | 131 | 155 | 162 | × 3 |

| 111 | 125 | × 4 |

Block Directory

The directory contains photographs and instructions for making 200 quilt blocks. Each block is graded by degree of difficulty, so you can choose the ones that suit your own skill level. For each block, there are also suggestions of three other blocks with which you could mix and match it to make a finished quilt.

CONSTRUCTION GUIDELINES

1 Snowball

Cut the following

Ⓐ One 6½in (16.2cm) square.
Ⓑ Four 2½in (6.2cm) squares.

Construction

 Sew a small square to a corner of the large square using the fast corners method (see page 113). Repeat this process at the remaining three corners.

Mix and match

2 Four-patch Chain

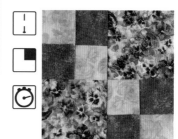

Cut the following

Ⓐ Four 2in (5cm) squares.
Ⓑ Four 2in (5cm) squares.
Ⓒ Two 3½in (8.7cm) squares.

Construction

Four-patch, see 13

Quick tip

Cut 2in (5cm) wide strips of fabrics A and B and sew them together before cutting crossways to make pairs of 2in (5cm) squares (see page 110).

Mix and match

3 Hourglass Variation

Cut the following

Ⓐ One 4⅛in (10.4cm) square cut into quarters diagonally to give four triangles.
Ⓑ One 4⅛in (10.4cm) square cut into quarters diagonally to give four triangles.
Ⓒ Two 3½in (8.7cm) squares.

Construction

Four X, see 63
Four-patch, see 13

Mix and match

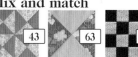

4 Old Maid's Puzzle

Cut the following

Ⓐ Four 2in (5cm) squares.

Ⓐ Five 2⅜in (5.8cm) squares cut in half diagonally to give ten triangles.

Ⓑ Two 2⅜in (5.8cm) squares cut in half diagonally to give four triangles.

Ⓒ One 2⅜in (5.8cm) square cut in half diagonally to give two triangles.

Ⓓ One 3⅞in (9.5cm) square cut in half diagonally to give two triangles.

Construction

Half-square Triangles, see 27
Bird in the Air, see 110
Four-patch, see 13

Quick tip

Chain piece the half-square triangles first (see page 110).

Mix and match

5 Diamond Four-patch

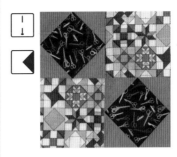

Cut the following

Ⓐ Two 3½in (8.7cm) squares.
Ⓑ Two 2⅝in (6.5cm) squares.
Ⓒ Four 2⅜in (5.8cm) squares cut in half diagonally to give eight triangles.

Construction

Diamond in the Square, see 86
Four-patch, see 13

Mix and match

6 Grandmother's Choice

Cut the following

Ⓐ Four 2⅛in (5.4cm) squares cut in half diagonally to give eight triangles.

Ⓑ Four 2⅞ x 1⅝in (7.2 x 4.2cm) strips.

Ⓒ Two 3⅛in (8cm) squares cut in half diagonally to give four triangles.

Ⓒ Five 1⅝in (4.2cm) squares.

Construction

Bird in the Air, see 110
Nine-patch, see 51

Mix and match

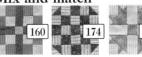

7 Birds in the Air

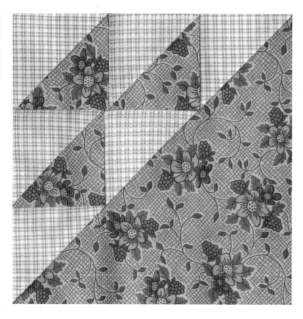

Cut the following

Ⓐ Three 2⅞in (7.2cm) squares cut in half diagonally to give six triangles.

Ⓑ Two 2⅞in (7.2cm) squares cut in half diagonally to give four triangles; you need three of them.

Ⓑ One 6⅞in (17cm) square cut in half diagonally to give two triangles; you need one of them.

Construction

Bird in the Air, see 110

Sew the five remaining small triangles together to form the central diagonal strip.

Half-square Triangles, see 27

Mix and match

8 Arrow

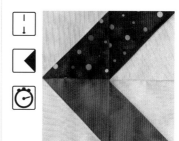

Cut the following

Ⓐ One 3⅞in (9.5cm) square cut in half diagonally to give two triangles.

Ⓑ One 3⅞in (9.5cm) square cut in half diagonally to give two triangles.

Ⓒ Two 3⅞in (9.5cm) squares cut in half diagonally to give four triangles.

Construction

Half-square Triangles, see 27
Four-patch, see 13

Mix and match

9 Economy

Cut the following

Ⓐ Two 3⅞in (9.5cm) squares cut in half diagonally to give four triangles.

Ⓑ One 4⅛in (10.4cm) square cut into quarters diagonally to give four triangles.

Ⓒ One 3½in (8.7cm) square.

Construction

Diamond in the Square, see 86

Quick tip

If you have trouble getting this block accurate, try adding an extra ¼in (6mm) to all the squares that will be cut into triangles and then trimming the block to size at each stage. Remember to leave the regular ¼in (6mm) seam allowance when you trim the finished block, though.

Mix and match

10 Diagonal Stripes

Cut the following

Ⓐ One 9¾ x 2⅝in (24.1 x 6.5cm) strip; trim both ends at a 45-degree angle.

Ⓐ One 3¾in (9.5cm) square cut in half diagonally to give two triangles; you need one of them.

Ⓑ One 9¾ x 2⅝in (24.1 x 6.5cm) strip; trim both ends at a 45-degree angle.

Ⓑ One 3¾in (9.5cm) square cut in half diagonally to give two triangles; you need one of them.

Construction

Sew one triangle to an alternate coloured strip.

Sew the remaining triangle and strip together.
Half-square Triangles, see 27

Quick tip

Take care not to stretch the long seam when pressing. To make the block more accurate, increase the size of the triangles by ¼in (6mm) and trim the block to size when complete, remembering to leave the regular ¼in (6mm) seam allowance.

Mix and match

27   36   80

11 Xquisite

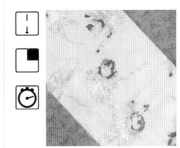

Cut the following

Ⓐ One 6½in (16.2cm) square.
Ⓑ Two 3in (7.6cm) squares.

Construction

Snowball, see 1

Mix and match

1   27   63

12 Mohawk Trail

Cut the following

Ⓐ Ⓑ Ⓒ Ⓓ

Ⓐ One piece using template 12a.
Ⓑ One piece using template 12a.
Ⓒ One piece using template 12a.
Ⓓ One piece using template 12b.

Construction

Join the three wedges together, matching the edges carefully.
Sew the curved piece in place.

Quick tip

See page 111 if you are unfamiliar with sewing curves.

Mix and match

1   54   96

CONSTRUCTION GUIDELINES

13 Four-patch

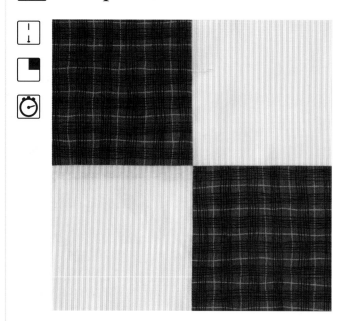

Cut the following

(A) Two 3⅜in (8.7cm) squares.

(B) Two 3⅜in (8.7cm) squares.

Construction

Join the squares into pairs of alternate colours.

Rotate the units, matching the centre points carefully, and then sew together.

14 Roman Square

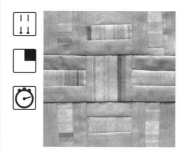

Cut the following

(A) Sixteen 2½ x 1⅛in (6.2 x 2.9cm) strips.

(B) Eight 2½ x 1⅛in (6.2 x 2.9cm) strips.

(B) One 2½in (6.2cm) square.

Construction

Stripes, see 99

Nine-patch, see 51

Quick tip

Cut two long 1⅛in (2.9cm) wide strips of fabric A and one long strip of fabric B. Sew the three strips together before cutting crossways into 2½in (6.2cm) segments.

15 Squares and Pinwheels

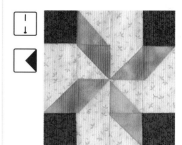

Cut the following

(A) Four 2in (5cm) squares.

(B) Four 2in (5cm) squares.

(B) Four 2⅜in (5.8cm) squares cut in half diagonally to give eight triangles.

(C) Four 2⅜in (5.8cm) squares cut in half diagonally to give eight triangles.

Construction

Half-square Triangles, see 27

Four-patch, see 13

Mix and match

 123 139 157

Mix and match

 81 94  108

Mix and match

43 58 59

16 Spinning Tops Variation

Cut the following

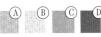

Ⓐ One 1⅝in (4.2cm) square.

Ⓑ Four 1⅝in (4.2cm) squares.

Ⓑ Four 2⅛in (5.4cm) squares cut in half diagonally to give eight triangles.

Ⓒ Four 1⅝in (4.2cm) squares.

Ⓓ Four 1⅝in (4.2cm) squares.

Ⓓ Two 3⅛in (8cm) squares cut in half diagonally to give four triangles.

Construction

Bird in the Air, see 110

Sew five squares together to form the horizontal centre strip.

Sew the remaining squares together in pairs.

Join the units to form the top and bottom rows. Join the rows to complete the block.

Mix and match

6   150   160

17 Ribbon Star

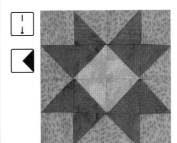

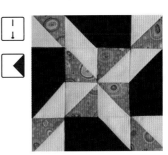

Cut the following

Ⓐ Four 2in (5cm) squares.

Ⓐ Four 2⅜in (5.8cm) squares cut in half diagonally to give eight triangles.

Ⓑ Six 2⅜in (5.8cm) squares cut in half diagonally to give twelve triangles.

Ⓒ Two 2⅜in (5.8cm) squares cut in half diagonally to give four triangles.

Construction

Half-square Triangles, see 27

Four-patch, see 13

Mix and match

103   114   168

18 Pinwheels

Cut the following

Ⓐ Four 2in (5cm) squares.

Ⓐ Two 2⅜in (5.8cm) squares cut in half diagonally to give four triangles.

Ⓑ Four 2⅜in (5.8cm) squares cut in half diagonally to give eight triangles.

Ⓒ Six 2⅜in (5.8cm) squares cut in half diagonally to give twelve triangles.

Construction

Half-square Triangles, see 27

Four-patch, see 13

Mix and match

121   126   162

19 Northwind

Cut the following

Ⓐ Three 2⅞in (7.2cm) squares cut in half diagonally to give six triangles; you need five of them.

Ⓐ One 4⅞in (12cm) square cut in half diagonally to give two triangles; you need one of them.

Ⓑ Three 2⅞in (7.2cm) squares cut in half diagonally to give six triangles; you need five of them.

Ⓑ One 4⅞in (12cm) square cut in half diagonally to give two triangles; you need one of them.

Construction

Join the small triangles to form two diagonal rows.

Sew these together to create the middle section.

Add a large triangle to either side to complete the block.

---

20 X Quartet

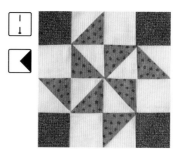

Cut the following

Ⓐ Four 2in (5cm) squares.

Ⓑ Four 2in (5cm) squares.

Ⓑ Four 2⅜in (5.8cm) squares cut in half diagonally to give eight triangles.

Ⓒ Four 2⅜in (5.8cm) squares cut in half diagonally to give eight triangles.

Construction

Half-square Triangles, see 27
Four-patch, see 13

---

21 Nelson's Victory

Cut the following

Ⓐ Ⓑ Ⓒ

Ⓐ Four 2in (5cm) squares.

Ⓑ Four 2in (5cm) squares.

Ⓑ Two 2⅜in (5.8cm) squares cut in half diagonally to give four triangles.

Ⓒ Four 2in (5cm) squares.

Ⓒ Two 2⅜in (5.8cm) squares cut in half diagonally to give four triangles.

Construction

Half-square Triangles, see 27
Four-patch, see 13

Mix and match

 7 10 16

Mix and match

 40 47 178

Mix and match

 59 164 192

22 Pinwheel

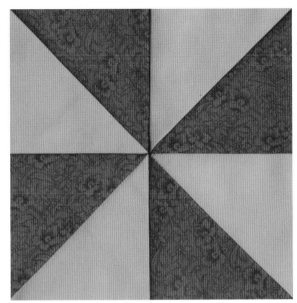

Cut the following

Ⓐ Two 3⅞in (9.5cm) squares cut in half diagonally to give four triangles.

Ⓑ Two 3⅞in (9.5cm) squares cut in half diagonally to give four triangles.

Construction

Half-square Triangles, see 27
Four-patch, see 13

Mix and match

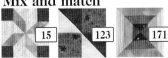
15 123 171

23 Eight Triangles

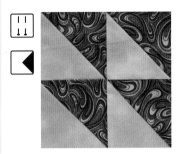

Cut the following

Ⓐ Ⓑ

Mix and match

2 141 161

24 Hopscotch Variation

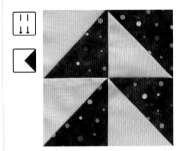

Cut the following

Ⓐ Ⓑ

Mix and match

13 111 145

25 Colorado Quilt Variation

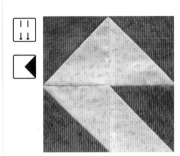

Cut the following

Ⓐ Ⓑ

Mix and match

5 54 73

26 Yankee Puzzle Variation

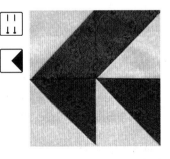

Cut the following

Ⓐ Ⓑ

Mix and match

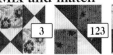
3 123 161

CONSTRUCTION GUIDELINES

27 Half-square Triangles

Cut the following

 Ⓐ Ⓑ

Ⓐ One 6⅞in (17cm) square cut in half diagonally to give two triangles; you need one of them.

Ⓑ One 6⅞in (17cm) square cut in half diagonally to give two triangles; you need one of them.

Quick tip

To prevent distortion of the bias edges, cut the squares ⅛in (3mm) bigger than specified and leave them whole. Place the squares right sides together, draw a pencil line along the diagonal and sew ¼in (6mm) either side of the drawn line (see page 113). Cut along the drawn line to make two blocks.

Construction

 Sew the triangles together along their long sides.

Mix and match

7   19   22

---

28 Broken Dishes

Cut the following

 Ⓐ Ⓑ Ⓒ

Ⓐ One 3⅞in (9.5cm) square cut in half diagonally to give two triangles.

Ⓑ One 3⅞in (9.5cm) square cut in half diagonally to give two triangles.

Ⓒ Two 3⅞in (9.5cm) squares cut in half diagonally to give four triangles.

Construction

Half-square Triangles, see 27

Four-patch, see 13

Mix and match

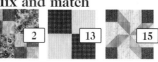
2   13   15

---

29 Shoofly

Cut the following

 Ⓐ Ⓑ

Ⓐ Two 2⅞in (7.2cm) squares cut in half diagonally to give four triangles.

Ⓐ Four 2½in (6.2cm) squares.

Ⓑ Two 2⅞in (7.2cm) squares cut in half diagonally to give four triangles.

Ⓑ One 2½in (6.2cm) square.

Construction

Half-square Triangles, see 27

Nine-patch, see 51

Mix and match

44   62   81

30 | Right and Left

Cut the following

Ⓐ One 4¼in (10.4cm) square cut into quarters diagonally to give four triangles.

Ⓑ One 4¼in (10.4cm) square cut into quarters diagonally to give four triangles; you need two of them.

Ⓒ One 4¼in (10.4cm) square cut into quarters diagonally to give four triangles; you need two of them.

Ⓓ One 4⅝in (11.8cm) square.

Construction

Join the triangles into pairs, matching the short edges.

Diamond in the Square, see 86

31 | Tile Puzzle

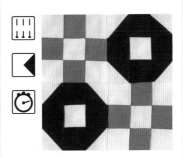

Cut the following

Ⓐ Eight 1½in (3.7cm) squares.

Ⓐ Four 1⅞in (4.7cm) squares cut in half diagonally to give eight triangles.

Ⓑ Twelve 1½in (3.7cm) squares.

Ⓑ Four 1⅞in (4.7cm) squares cut in half diagonally to give eight triangles.

Ⓒ Eight 1½in (3.7cm) squares.

Construction

Half-square Triangles, see 27

Nine-patch, see 51

Four-patch, see 13

32 | Crockett Cabin Quilt

Cut the following

Ⓐ Four 2in (5cm) squares.

Ⓐ Two 2⅜in (5.8cm) squares cut in half diagonally to give four triangles.

Ⓑ Eight 2in (5cm) squares.

Ⓑ Two 2⅜in (5.8cm) squares cut in half diagonally to give four triangles.

Construction

Half-square Triangles, see 27

Four-patch, see 13

Mix and match

 15 24 86

Mix and match

 34 36 38

Mix and match

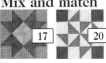 17  20 40

33 Cockscomb

Cut the following

A Two 4¼in (10.4cm) squares cut into quarters diagonally to give eight triangles; you need six of them.

A One 2¾in (6.8cm) square cut into quarters diagonally to give four triangles.

A Two 1½in (3.7cm) squares.

B One 4¼in (10.4cm) square cut into quarters diagonally to give four triangles.

B One 2¾in (6.8cm) square cut into quarters diagonally to give four triangles.

C One 4¼in (10.4cm) square cut into quarters diagonally to give four triangles; you need two of them.

C Two 1½in (3.7cm) squares.

Construction

Join two small triangles to each square in the correct colour combinations.

Add three large triangles on one side of the pieced units to create each quarter of the block. Four X, see 63

Mix and match

86 88 188

34 Miller's Daughter

Cut the following

A Two 3½in (8.7cm) squares.

B Sixteen 1¼in (3.1cm) squares.

C Eight 2 x 1¼in (5 x 3.1cm) strips.

D Two 2in (5cm) squares.

Construction

Snowball, see 1
Nine-patch, see 51
Four-patch, see 13

Mix and match

35 38 58

35 Around the Twist

Cut the following

A Two 3½in (8.7cm) squares.

A Two 2in (5cm) squares.

B Four 2¾ x 1¼in (6.8 x 3.1cm) strips.

B Four 1¼in (3.1cm) squares.

C Four 2¾ x 1¼in (6.8 x 3.1cm) strips.

C Four 1¼in (3.1cm) squares.

Construction

Snowball, see 1
Bright Hopes, see 39
Four-patch, see 13

Mix and match

31 34 78

36 Indian Hatchet

Cut the following

Ⓐ Four 5½ x 1½in
(14 x 3.7cm) strips.

Ⓑ Four 3⅛in (7.7cm) squares
cut in half diagonally to give
eight triangles.

Repeat this process to make
three more units.
Four-patch, see 13

Construction

 Mark the midpoint
of one strip and the
long sides of two
triangles with a small crease.
Sew a triangle to each side
of the strip, matching up the
crease marks, and then trim
the strip level with the sides
of the triangles.

Mix and match

13 28 80

37 Double Quartet

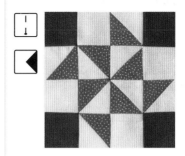

Cut the following

Ⓐ Four 2in (5cm) squares.

Ⓑ Four 2in (5cm) squares.

Ⓑ Four 2⅜in (5.8cm) squares
cut in half diagonally to give
eight triangles.

Ⓒ Four 2⅜in (5.8cm) squares
cut in half diagonally to give
eight triangles.

Construction

Half-square Triangles, see 27
Four-patch, see 13

Mix and match

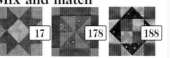
17 178 188

38 Delaware's Flagstone

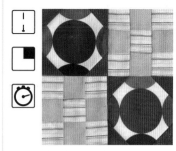

Cut the following

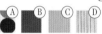

Ⓐ Two 3⅜in (8.7cm) squares.

Ⓑ Eight 1½in (3.7cm) squares.

Ⓒ Eight 1½in (3.7cm) squares.

Ⓓ Ten 1½in (3.7cm) squares.

Construction

Snowball, see 1
Nine-patch, see 51
Four-patch, see 13

Mix and match

31 34 132

CONSTRUCTION GUIDELINES

39 Bright Hopes

Cut the following

(A) One 2½in (6.2cm) square.
(B) One 4½ x 2½in
(11.2 x 6.2cm) strip.
(C) One 4½ x 2½in
(11.2 x 6.2cm) strip.
(D) One 4½ x 2½in
(11.2 x 6.2cm) strip.
(E) One 4½ x 2½in
(11.2 x 6.2cm) strip.

Construction

 Aligning one end of a strip with the edge of the square, sew together and press flat.

 Place the next strip across the end of the square and the previous strip. Sew in place.

 Repeat this process to add the third strip.

Add the final strip in the same way, then sew the remaining edges of the first and final strips together.

Mix and match

 83 85 102

40 Free Trade

Cut the following

(A) Six 2in (5cm) squares.
(A) Five 2⅜in (5.8cm) squares cut in half diagonally to give ten triangles.
(B) Five 2⅜in (5.8cm) squares cut in half diagonally to give ten triangles.

Construction

Half-square Triangles, see 27
Four-patch, see 13

Mix and match

  20 47 61

41 Cracker

Cut the following

(A) One 3⅞in (9.5cm) square cut in half diagonally to give two triangles.
(A) Two 4¾ x 1⅞in (11.8 x 4.7cm) strips.
(B) One 3⅞in (9.5cm) square cut in half diagonally to give two triangles.
(B) One 4¾ x 1⅞in (11.8 x 4.7cm) strip.

Construction

Stripes, see 99
Diamond in the Square, see 86

Mix and match

  13 15 22

42 Lucky Clover

Cut the following

Ⓐ Six 1½in (3.7cm) squares.
Ⓑ Six 1½in (3.7cm) squares.
Ⓒ Four 2⅞ x 1½in (7.2 x 3.7cm) strips; trim one end at a 45-degree angle.
Ⓓ Four 2⅞ x 1½in (7.2 x 3.7cm) strips; trim one end at a 45-degree angle.
Ⓔ Eight 2⅞ x 1½in (7.2 x 3.7cm) strips; trim one end at a 45-degree angle.

Do not sew into the seam allowances at the inner angles.

Inset the small squares to complete each quarter of the block.
Four-patch, see 13

Quick tip
Lay out the pieces before sewing in order to ensure correct placement. Steam can help if this block does not lay flat at first.

Construction

Sew pairs of angled segments together in the correct colour combinations.

Mix and match

  48 50 59

43 Whirling Blade

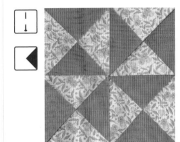

Cut the following

Ⓐ Ⓑ

Ⓐ Two 4¼in (10.4cm) squares cut into quarters diagonally to give eight triangles.
Ⓑ Two 4¼in (10.4cm) squares cut into quarters diagonally to give eight triangles.

Construction
Four X, see 63
Four-patch, see 13

Mix and match

 18 55 56

44 Jacks on Six

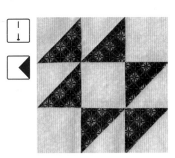

Cut the following

Ⓐ Ⓑ

Ⓐ Three 2½in (6.2cm) squares.
Ⓐ Three 2⅞in (7.2cm) squares cut in half diagonally to give six triangles.
Ⓑ Three 2⅞in (7.2cm) squares cut in half diagonally to give six triangles.

Construction
Half-square Triangles, see 27
Nine-patch, see 51

Mix and match

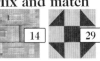 14 29 60

CONSTRUCTION GUIDELINES

45 Spool

Cut the following

 Ⓐ Ⓑ

Ⓐ One 2⅜in (6.2cm) square.

Ⓐ Two 7¼ x 2⅜in
(17.9 x 6.2cm) strips;
trim each end at a
45-degree angle.

Ⓑ Two 7¼ x 2⅜in
(17.9 x 6.2cm) strips;
trim each end at a
45-degree angle.

Construction

 Sew two matching coloured angled pieces to opposite sides of the square. Do not sew into the seam allowances. Add the alternate coloured sections to the remaining sides of the square. Do not sew through the seam allowances and pivot at the corner points (see page 111).

Mix and match

---

46 Antique Tile

Cut the following

 Ⓐ Ⓑ Ⓒ

Ⓐ One 2½in (6.2cm) square.

Ⓐ Four 1½in (3.7cm) squares.

Ⓐ Four 2½ x 1½in
(6.2 x 3.7cm) strips.

Ⓑ Four 2½ x 1½in
(6.2 x 3.7cm) strips.

Ⓑ Four 1½in (3.7cm) squares.

Ⓒ Four 2½ x 1½in
(6.2 x 3.7cm) strips.

Construction

Stripes, see 99

Four-patch, see 13

Nine-patch, see 51

Mix and match

 14 100 130

---

47 Barbara Frietschie

Cut the following

Ⓐ Ⓑ Ⓒ Ⓓ Ⓔ

Ⓐ Four 2⅜in (5.8cm) squares cut in half diagonally to give eight triangles.

Ⓑ Six 2⅜in (5.8cm) squares cut in half diagonally to give twelve triangles.

Ⓒ Two 2⅜in (5.8cm) squares cut in half diagonally to give four triangles.

Ⓓ Two 2⅜in (5.8cm) squares cut in half diagonally to give four triangles.

Ⓔ Two 2⅜in (5.8cm) squares cut in half diagonally to give four triangles.

Construction

Half-square Triangles, see 27

Four-patch, see 13

Mix and match

 103 111 114

48 Eight-pointed Star

Cut the following

Ⓐ Four 2⅛in (5.6cm) squares.

Ⓐ One 3⅝in (9.3cm) square cut into quarters diagonally to give four triangles.

Ⓑ Eight pieces using template 48a.

Construction

 Join the diamond shapes into pairs, making sure you do not sew through the seam allowances at each end.

 Insert the squares at the corners where the diamonds meet, sewing from the inner angle of the diamonds out towards the edges of the squares each time. Repeat to add the triangles, first sewing the diamonds together and then inserting the triangles.

Mix and match

17   162   183

---

49 Road to Oklahoma

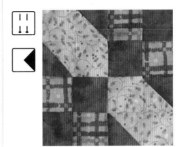

Cut the following

Ⓐ Four 2in (5cm) squares.

Ⓑ Four 2in (5cm) squares.

Ⓑ Two 2⅜in (5.8cm) squares cut in half diagonally to give four triangles.

Ⓒ Four 2in (5cm) squares.

Ⓒ Two 2⅜in (5.8cm) squares cut in half diagonally to give four triangles.

Construction

Half-square Triangles, see 27
Four-patch, see 13

Mix and match

28   58   73

---

50 Grandmother's Cross

Cut the following

Ⓐ Ten 1½in (3.7cm) squares.

Ⓑ Ten 1½in (3.7cm) squares.

Ⓒ Two 2⅜in (5.8cm) squares cut in half diagonally to give four triangles.

Ⓓ One 4⅛in (10.4cm) square cut into quarters diagonally to give four triangles.

Construction

Four-patch, see 13
Mosaic, see 147

Mix and match

16   33   147

CONSTRUCTION GUIDELINES

51 Nine-patch

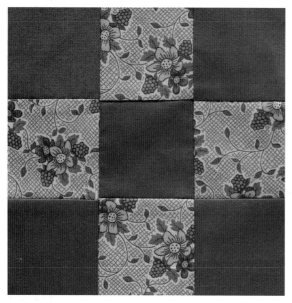

Cut the following

A Five 2½in (6.2cm) squares.
B Four 2½in (6.2cm) squares.

Construction

 Lay out the nine squares in the correct order. Starting at the top left and working downward, chain piece pairs of squares together without cutting the thread (see page 110).

 Add another square to each pair in the same way so that you have three rows of three squares. Join the rows.

Mix and match

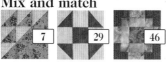 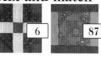
7 29 46

52 Counterpane

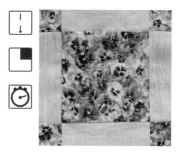

Cut the following

Ⓐ Four 1½in (3.7cm) squares.
Ⓐ One 4½in (11.2cm) square.
Ⓑ Four 4½ x 1½in (11.2 x 3.7cm) strips.

Construction

Nine-patch, see 51

Mix and match

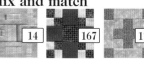
6 87 166

53 Virginia Worm Fence

Cut the following

Ⓐ Nine 2½ x 1½in (6.2 x 3.7cm) strips.
Ⓑ Nine 2½ x 1½in (6.2 x 3.7cm) strips.

Construction

Stripes, see 99
Nine-patch, see 51

Quick tip

Sew long 1½in (3.7cm) wide strips of alternate coloured fabrics together before cutting crossways into 2½in (6.2cm) segments.

Mix and match

14 167 172

54 Sunrise Sunset

Cut the following

Ⓐ One piece using template 54a.
Ⓑ One piece using template 54b.
Ⓒ One piece using template 54c.
Ⓓ One piece using template 54d.

Construction

 Start with the quarter circle section and add the first ring. Mark the centre of the adjoining edges with a small crease and pin together at this point. Pin the rest of the curved edges together and then sew the seam, easing the curve into place.

 Repeat to add the next ring. There is no need to snip the curved seam allowances. Add the final curved piece in the same way.

Quick tip

Add an extra ¼in (6mm) seam allowance to the outer straight edges of piece 54d and trim to fit when sewn in place.

Mix and match

 96   180   185

55 Eccentric Star

Cut the following

 Ⓐ Ⓑ Ⓒ

Ⓐ One 2½in (6.2cm) square.
Ⓑ Four 2⅞in (7.2cm) squares cut in half diagonally to give eight triangles.
Ⓒ Four 2⅞in (7.2cm) squares cut in half diagonally to give eight triangles.

Construction

Half-square Triangles, see 27
Nine-patch, see 51

Mix and match

152   169   186

56 Caroline's Choice

Cut the following

 Ⓐ Ⓑ Ⓒ

Ⓐ One 4¼in (10.4cm) square cut into quarters diagonally to give four triangles.
Ⓑ One 4¼in (10.4cm) square cut into quarters diagonally to give four triangles.
Ⓑ Four 2⅜in (5.8cm) squares cut in half diagonally to give eight triangles.
Ⓒ Four 2⅜in (5.8cm) squares cut in half diagonally to give eight triangles.

Construction

Half-square Triangles, see 27
Four X, see 63
Four-patch, see 13

Mix and match

 111   164   190

57 Cups and Saucers

Cut the following

Ⓐ Four 2½ x 1½in (6.2 x 3.7cm) strips.

Ⓐ Two 2⅞in (7.2cm) squares cut in half diagonally to give four triangles.

Ⓑ Four 2½ x 1½in (6.2 x 3.7cm) strips.

Ⓒ Four 1½in (3.7cm) squares.

Ⓒ One 2⅞in (7.2cm) square cut in half diagonally to give two triangles; you need one of them.

Ⓓ Four 1½in (3.7cm) squares.

Ⓓ One 2⅞in (7.2cm) square cut in half diagonally to give two triangles; you need one of them.

Ⓔ Four 1½in (3.7cm) squares.

Ⓔ One 2⅞in (7.2cm) square cut in half diagonally to give two triangles; you need one of them.

Ⓕ Four 1½in (3.7cm) squares.

Ⓕ One 2⅞in (7.2cm) square cut in half diagonally to give two triangles; you need one of them.

Ⓖ One 2½in (6.2cm) square.

Construction

Half-square Triangles, see 27
Fast Geese, see 134
Nine-patch, see 51

Mix and match

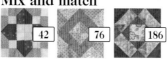

58 Indiana Puzzle

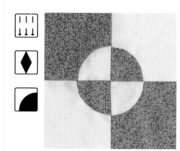

Cut the following

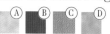

Ⓐ Two pieces using template 58a.

Ⓐ Two pieces using template 58b.

Ⓑ Two pieces using template 58a.

Ⓑ Two pieces using template 58b.

Construction

Drunkard's Path, see 122
Four-patch, see 13

Mix and match

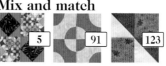

59 Carrie Nation Quilt

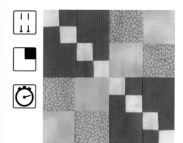

Cut the following

Ⓐ Eight 1¼in (3.1cm) squares.

Ⓑ Eight 1¼in (3.1cm) squares.

Ⓑ Four 2in (5cm) squares.

Ⓒ Four 2in (5cm) squares.

Ⓓ Four 2in (5cm) squares.

Construction

Four-patch, see 13

Mix and match

60 Hourglass I

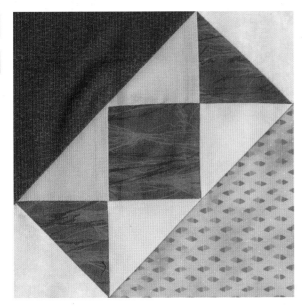

Cut the following

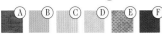

Ⓐ One 2½in (6.2cm) square.

Ⓐ One 2⅞in (7.2cm) square cut in half diagonally to give two triangles.

Ⓑ One 2⅞in (7.2cm) square cut in half diagonally to give two triangles.

Ⓒ One 2⅞in (7.2cm) square cut in half diagonally to give two triangles.

Ⓓ One 2⅞in (7.2cm) square cut in half diagonally to give two triangles.

Ⓔ One 4¾in (12cm) square cut in half diagonally to give two triangles; you need one of them.

Ⓕ One 4¾in (12cm) square cut in half diagonally to give two triangles; you need one of them.

Construction

 Join the square and small triangles into units of three, then sew together to create the centre diagonal section. Add the two large triangles to either side.

61 Four X Quilt

 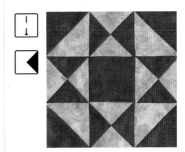

Cut the following

Ⓐ One 2½in (6.2cm) square.

Ⓐ Two 3¼in (8cm) squares cut into quarters diagonally to give eight triangles.

Ⓐ Two 2⅞in (7.2cm) squares cut in half diagonally to give four triangles.

Ⓑ Two 3¼in (8cm) squares cut into quarters diagonally to give eight triangles.

Ⓑ Two 2⅞in (7.2cm) squares cut in half diagonally to give four triangles.

Construction

Half-square Triangles, see ⎡27⎤
Four X, see ⎡63⎤
Nine-patch, see ⎡51⎤

62 Spider

Cut the following

Ⓐ Five 2⅞in (7.2cm) squares cut in half diagonally to give ten triangles; you need nine of them.

Ⓑ Three 2⅞in (7.2cm) squares cut in half diagonally to give six triangles.

Ⓒ Two 2⅞in (7.2cm) squares cut in half diagonally to give four triangles; you need three of them.

Construction

Half-square Triangles, see ⎡27⎤
Nine-patch, see ⎡51⎤

Mix and match
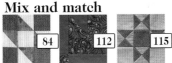 84 112 115

Mix and match
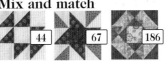 44 67 186

Mix and match
   68 108 169

CONSTRUCTION GUIDELINES

63 Four X

Cut the following

 (A) (B)

(A) One 7¼in (17.9cm) square cut into quarters diagonally to give four triangles; you need two of them.

(B) One 7¼in (17.9cm) square cut into quarters diagonally to give four triangles; you need two of them.

 Repeat to make a second pair of triangles.
Join the two sections together, making sure the centre points are sharp.

Quick tip

For more accurate piecing when sewing triangles, see page 113.

Construction

 Sew a pair of alternate coloured triangles together along their short sides.

Mix and match

 13 15 24

64 Hourglass II

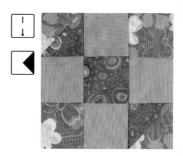

Cut the following

(A) (B) (C)

(A) One 2½in (6.2cm) square.

(A) One 2⅞in (7.2cm) square cut in half diagonally to give two triangles.

(B) Two 2½in (6.2cm) squares.

(B) One 2⅞in (7.2cm) square cut in half diagonally to give two triangles.

(C) Four 2½in (6.2cm) squares.

Construction

Half-square Triangles, see 27
Nine-patch, see 51

Mix and match

 44 67 84

65 Home Queen

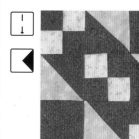

Cut the following

(A) (B) (C)

(A) Two 2½in (6.2cm) squares.

(A) Two 2⅞in (7.2cm) squares cut in half diagonally to give four triangles.

(A) Six 1½in (3.7cm) squares.

(B) Two 2⅞in (7.2cm) squares cut in half diagonally to give four triangles.

(C) Six 1½in (3.7cm) squares.

Construction

Four-patch, see 13
Half-square Triangles, see 27
Nine-patch, see 51

Mix and match

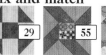 29 55 64

66 Double Monkey Wrench

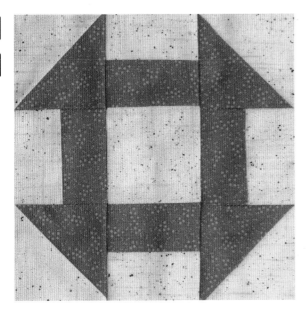

Cut the following

Ⓐ Two 2⅞in (7.2cm) squares cut in half diagonally to give four triangles.

Ⓐ One 2½in (6.2cm) square.

Ⓐ Four 2½ x 1½in (6.2 x 3.7cm) strips.

Ⓑ Two 2⅞in (7.2cm) squares cut in half diagonally to give four triangles.

Ⓑ Four 2½ x 1½in (6.2 x 3.7cm) strips.

Construction

Half-square Triangles, see 27

Stripes, see 99

Nine-patch, see 51

---

67 Eccentric Star Variation

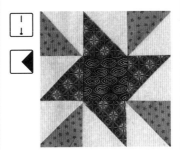

Cut the following

Ⓐ One 2½in (6.2cm) square.

Ⓑ Two 2⅞in (7.2cm) squares cut in half diagonally to give four triangles.

Ⓒ Two 2⅞in (7.2cm) squares cut in half diagonally to give four triangles.

Ⓓ Four 2⅞in (7.2cm) squares cut in half diagonally to give eight triangles.

Construction

Half-square Triangles, see 27

Nine-patch, see 51

---

68 Double X

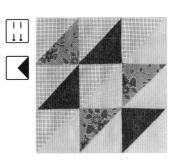

Cut the following

Ⓐ Three 2⅞in (7.2cm) squares cut in half diagonally to give six triangles.

Ⓑ Three 2⅞in (7.2cm) squares cut in half diagonally to give six triangles.

Ⓒ Two 2⅞in (7.2cm) squares cut in half diagonally to give four triangles; you need three of them.

Ⓓ Three 2⅞in (7.2cm) squares cut in half diagonally to give four triangles; you need three of them.

Construction

Half-square Triangles, see 27

Nine-patch, see 51

Mix and match

7   44   45

Mix and match

61   77   94

Mix and match

27   153   163

69 Kaleidoscope

Cut the following

(A) Four pieces using template 69a.
(B) Four pieces using template 69a.
(B) Two 2⅝in (6.5cm) squares cut in half diagonally to give four triangles.

Construction

Starry Night, see 183 Fold the centre unit in half along both diagonals and mark the edges with a small crease. Fold each triangle in half and mark the centre of the long edges with a small crease. Sew a triangle to each corner of the block, aligning the creases.

---

70 Improved Four-patch

Cut the following

(A) Four 1½in (3.7cm) squares.
(B) Four 1½in (3.7cm) squares.
(C) Two 2⅝in (6.5cm) squares.
(D) Two 3⅞in (9.5cm) squares cut in half diagonally to give four triangles.

Construction

Four-patch, see 13
Diamond in the Square, see 86

---

71 New Album

Cut the following

(A) One 3in (7.6cm) square.
(A) Four 4 x 1⅝in (10.2 x 4.2cm) strips.
(B) Four 1⅝in (4.2cm) squares.
(B) Two 2⅝in (6.5cm) squares cut in half diagonally to give four triangles.

Construction

Diamond in the Square, see 86
Nine-patch, see 51

Mix and match

1   115   183

Mix and match

86   136   188

Mix and match

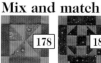

178   181   184

72 Arrowhead

Cut the following

Ⓐ Four 4 x 1½in (10 x 3.7cm) strips; trim one end at a 45-degree angle, matching the direction of the angles to the finished block.

Ⓐ Two 1½in (3.7cm) squares.

Ⓐ One 4¼in (10.4cm) square cut into quarters diagonally; you need two of them.

Ⓑ Four 4 x 1½in (10 x 3.7cm) strips; trim one end at a 45-degree angle, matching the direction of the angles to the finished block.

Ⓑ Two 1½in (3.7cm) squares.

Ⓑ One 4¼in (10.4cm) square cut into quarters diagonally; you need two of them.

Construction

Join the strips in pairs to create a point at the angled ends.

Sew the four-patch unit (see block 13).

Join a pair of strips to opposite sides of the four-patch unit.

Join a triangle to opposite sides of the remaining pairs of strips.
Sew the three sections together.

Mix and match

50   92   189

73 Monastery Windows

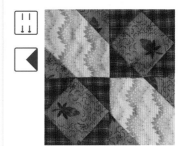

Cut the following

Ⓐ Two 2⅝in (6.5cm) squares.

Ⓐ Four 1¾in (4.2cm) squares.

Ⓑ Four 2⅜in (5.8cm) squares cut in half diagonally to give eight triangles.

Ⓒ Two 3½in (8.7cm) squares.

Construction

Diamond in the Square, see 86
Snowball, see 1
Four-patch, see 13

Mix and match

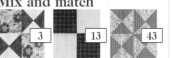

3   13   43

74 Windmill

Cut the following

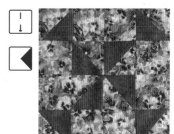

Ⓐ Eight 2in (5cm) squares.

Ⓐ Four 2⅜in (5.8cm) squares cut in half diagonally to give eight triangles.

Ⓑ Four 2⅜in (5.8cm) squares cut in half diagonally to give eight triangles.

Construction

Half-square Triangles, see 27
Four-patch, see 13

Mix and match

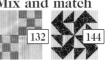

132   144   163

CONSTRUCTION GUIDELINES

75 Dutchman's Puzzle

Cut the following

Ⓐ Eight 2⅜in (5.8cm) squares cut in half diagonally to give sixteen triangles.

Ⓑ One 4¼in (10.4cm) square cut into quarters diagonally to give four triangles; you need two of them.

Ⓒ One 4¼in (10.4cm) square cut into quarters diagonally to give four triangles; you need two of them.

Ⓓ One 4¼in (10.4cm) square cut into quarters diagonally to give four triangles; you need two of them.

Ⓔ One 4¼in (10.4cm) square cut into quarters diagonally to give four triangles; you need two of them.

Construction

Sew the long sides of two small triangles to the two short sides of each large triangle.

Join pairs of units together, checking the colour placement.

Join the pieced squares into pairs, rotating them to form the pattern.
Join the two rows to complete the block.

Mix and match

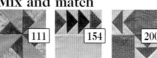

76 Blockade

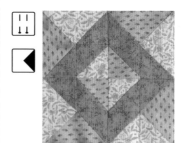

Cut the following

Ⓐ Six 2⅜in (5.8cm) squares cut in half diagonally to give twelve triangles.

Ⓑ Five 2⅜in (5.8cm) squares cut in half diagonally to give ten triangles.

Ⓒ One 2⅜in (5.8cm) square cut in half diagonally to give two triangles.

Ⓒ One 4¼in (10.4cm) square cut into quarters diagonally to give four triangles.

Construction

Dutchman's Puzzle, see 75
Half-square Triangles, see 27
Four-patch, see 13

Mix and match

77 Calico Puzzle

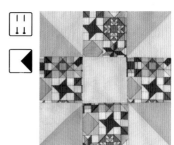

Cut the following

Ⓐ One 2½in (6.2cm) square.

Ⓐ Two 2⅞in (7.2cm) squares cut in half diagonally to give four triangles.

Ⓑ Two 2⅞in (7.2cm) squares cut in half diagonally to give four triangles.

Ⓒ Four 2½in (6.2cm) squares.

Construction

Half-square Triangles, see 27
Nine-patch, see 51

Mix and match

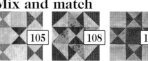

78 Flying Squares Variation

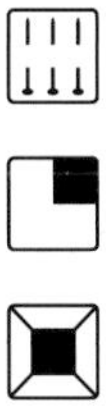

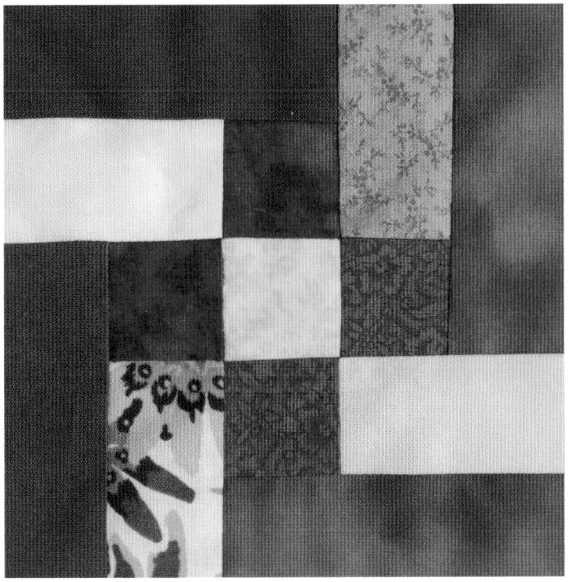

Cut the following

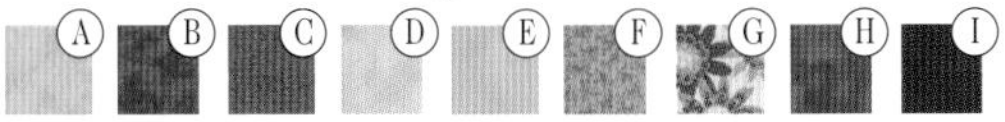
A
B
C
D
E
F
G
H
I

(A) One 1¾in (4.2cm) square.
(B) Two 1¾in (4.2cm) squares.
(C) Two 1¾in (4.2cm) squares.
(D) One 2⅞ x 1¾in (7.2 x 4.2cm) strip.
(E) One 2⅞ x 1¾in (7.2 x 4.2cm) strip.
(F) One 2⅞ x 1¾in (7.2 x 4.2cm) strip.
(G) One 2⅞ x 1¾in (7.2 x 4.2cm) strip.
(H) Two 4⅛ x 1¾in (10.2 x 4.2cm) strips.
(I) Two 4⅛ x 1⅛in (10.2 x 4.2cm) strips.

Construction

Sew a square to the end of each short strip in the correct colour combinations.

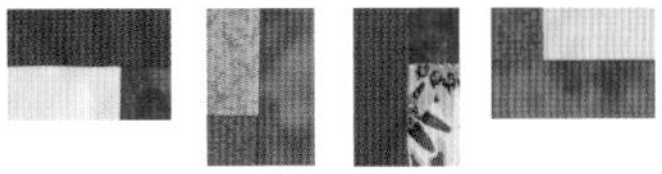

Join pairs of pieced units and long strips together.

Bright Hopes, see 39

Mix and match

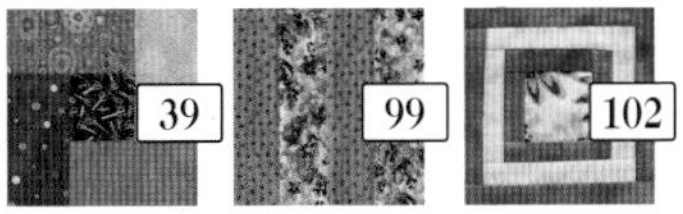
39
99
102

79 Mr Roosevelt's Necktie

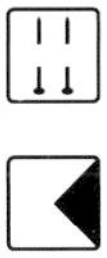

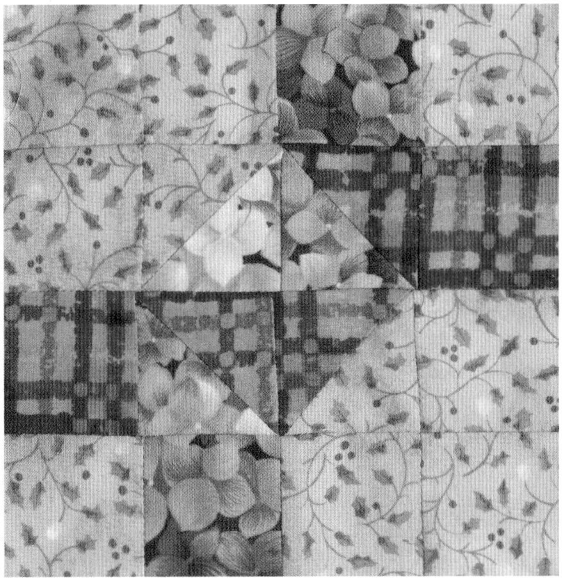

Cut the following

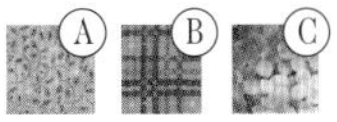
A
B
C

(A) Eight 2in (5cm) squares.
(A) One 2⅜in (5.8cm) square cut in half diagonally to give two triangles.
(B) Two 2in (5cm) squares.
(B) Two 2⅜in (5.8cm) squares cut in half diagonally to give four triangles; you need three of them.
(C) Two 2in (5cm) squares.
(C) Two 2⅜in (5.8cm) squares cut in half diagonally to give four triangles; you need three of them.

Construction

Half-square Triangles, see 27
Four-patch, see 13

Mix and match

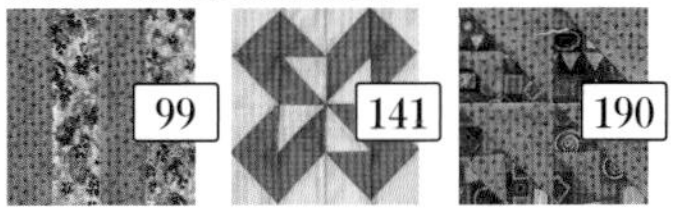
99
141
190

80 Diagonal Stripe

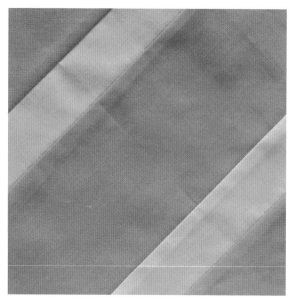

Cut the following

Ⓐ One 3⅜in (8.3cm) square cut in half diagonally to give two triangles.
Ⓐ One piece using template 80a.
Ⓑ Two 6⅞ x 1½in (17 x 3.7cm) strips; trim both ends at a 45-degree angle.

Construction

 Join each strip to a triangle, matching the centre points.
Join the triangle sections to opposite sides of the template piece, matching the centre points.

---

81 Steps to the Altar

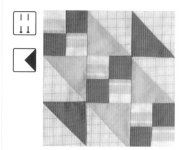

Cut the following

Ⓐ Six 1½in (3.7cm) squares.
Ⓐ One 2⅞in (7.2cm) square cut in half diagonally to give two triangles.
Ⓑ Six 1½in (3.7cm) squares.
Ⓒ Three 2⅞in (7.2cm) squares cut in half diagonally to give six triangles.
Ⓓ Two 2⅞in (7.2cm) squares cut in half diagonally to give four triangles.

Construction

Half-square Triangles, see 27
Four-patch, see 13
Nine-patch, see 51

---

82 Squares and Stripe

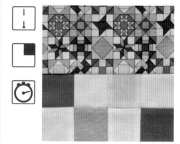

Cut the following

Ⓐ One 2in (5cm) square.
Ⓑ Four 2in (5cm) squares.
Ⓒ One 2in (5cm) square.
Ⓓ One 2in (5cm) square.
Ⓔ One 2in (5cm) square.
Ⓕ One 6½ x 3½in (16.2 x 8.7cm) strip.

Construction

Four-patch, see 13

Mix and match

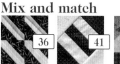

Mix and match

Mix and match

83 Bonnie Scotsman

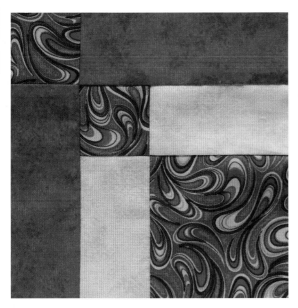

Cut the following

Ⓐ Two 2in (5cm) squares.

Ⓐ One 3½in (8.7cm) square.

Ⓑ Two 3½ x 2in
(8.7 x 5cm) strips.

Ⓒ Two 5 x 2in
(12.4 x 5cm) strips.

Construction

Join a small square to one of
the short strips.

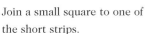

Repeat this process with one
of the longer strips.

Join the
remaining short
strip (without a
square) to the large square.

Add the matching
short strip with
its square.
Add the
remaining pieces in the same
way to complete the block.

Mix and match

84 Double Hourglass

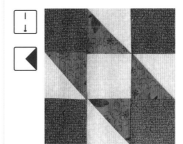

Cut the following

Ⓐ Four 2½in (6.2cm) squares.

Ⓑ One 2½in (6.2cm) square.

Ⓑ Two 2⅞in (7.2cm) squares
cut in half diagonally to give
four triangles.

Ⓒ Two 2⅞in (7.2cm) squares
cut in half diagonally to give
four triangles.

Construction

Half-square Triangles, see 27
Nine-patch, see 51

Mix and match

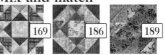

85 Uneven Stripes

Cut the following

Ⓐ One 6½ x 2⅞in
(16.2 x 7.2cm) strip.

Ⓐ One 6½ x 1⅜in
(16.2 x 4.2cm) strip.

Ⓑ Two 6½ x 1⅜in
(16.2 x 4.2cm) strips.

Construction

Stripes, see 99

Mix and match

CONSTRUCTION GUIDELINES

86 Diamond in the Square

Cut the following

 (A)   (B)

(A) One 4⅝in (11.8cm) square.
(B) Two 3¾in (9.5cm) squares cut in half diagonally to give four triangles.

Construction

Mark the middle of each side of the square with a small crease.
Do the same on the long side of each triangle. Lay a triangle onto one side of the square with creases matching and right sides together. Sew and then press open.

Repeat this process to add another triangle on the opposite side of the square.
Add the last two triangles to complete the block.

Mix and match

 56   63   76

87 Hourglass III

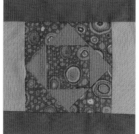

Cut the following

 (A)   (B)   (C)   (D)

(A) One 2½in (6.2cm) square.
(A) Two 2⅞in (7.2cm) squares cut in half diagonally to give four triangles.
(B) One 3¼in (8cm) square cut into quarters diagonally to give four triangles.
(C) Two 4½ x 1½in (11.2 x 3.7cm) strips.
(D) Two 6½ x 1½in (16.2 x 3.7cm) strips.

Construction

Diamond in the Square, see 86
Courthouse Steps, see 195

Mix and match

 178   184   194

88 Shoofly Variation

Cut the following

(A) (B)

(A) One 1¾in (4.2cm) square.
(A) Two 3¼in (8cm) squares cut in half diagonally to give four triangles.
(B) Four 2⅞ x 1¾in (7.2 x 4.2cm) strips.
(B) Two 3¼in (8cm) squares cut in half diagonally to give four triangles.

Construction

Half-square Triangles, see 27
Nine-patch, see 51

Mix and match

 109   131 160

89 Greek Cross

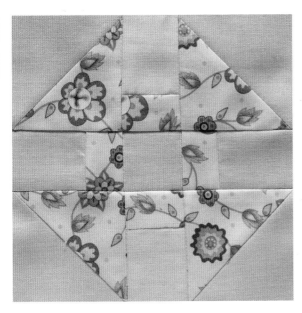

Cut the following

Ⓐ Two 3⅛in (8cm) squares cut in half diagonally to give four triangles.

Ⓐ Four 1¾ x 1¼in (4.2 x 3.1cm) strips.

Ⓑ Two 3⅛in (8cm) squares cut in half diagonally to give four triangles.

Ⓑ Four 2⅛ x 1⅝in (5.4 x 4.2cm) strips.

Ⓑ One 1⅝in (4.2cm) square.

Construction

 Sew a small strip to the end of each long strip.

 Half-square Triangles, see 27

Nine-patch, see 51

90 Grandma's Favourite

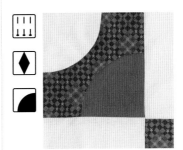

Cut the following

Ⓐ Ⓑ Ⓒ

Ⓐ Two 5¼ x 1⅝in (13.1 x 4.2cm) strips.

Ⓐ One piece using template 90a.

Ⓑ One 1⅝in (4.2cm) square.

Ⓑ One piece using template 90b.

Ⓒ One piece using template 90c.

Construction

Drunkard's Path, see 122

Four-patch, see 13

91 Steeplechase

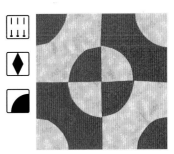

Cut the following

Ⓐ Ⓑ

Ⓐ Four pieces using template 91a.

Ⓐ Two pieces using template 91b.

Ⓑ Four pieces using template 91a.

Ⓑ Two pieces using template 91b.

Construction

Drunkard's Path, see 122

Four-patch, see 13

Mix and match

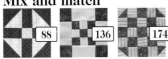

Mix and match

Mix and match

92 Diagonal Four-patch Chain

Cut the following

Ⓐ One 3⅞in (9.5cm) square
cut in half diagonally to give
two triangles.

Ⓑ One 3⅞in (9.5cm) square
cut in half diagonally to give
two triangles.

Ⓑ Four 2in (5cm) squares.

Ⓒ Four 2in (5cm) squares.

Construction

Half-square Triangles, see 27
Four-patch, see 13

Mix and match

4   114   123

93 Sickle

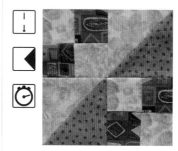

Cut the following

Ⓐ Ⓑ Ⓒ

Mix and match

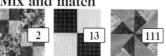
2   13   111

94 Roman Stripe

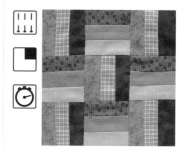

Cut the following

Ⓐ Ⓑ Ⓒ Ⓓ Ⓔ Ⓕ

Ⓐ Five 2½ x 1⅛in
(6.2 x 2.9cm) strips.

Ⓑ Five 2½ x 1⅛in
(6.2 x 2.9cm) strips.

Ⓒ Five 2½ x 1⅛in
(6.2 x 2.9cm) strips.

Ⓓ Four 2½ x 1⅛in
(6.2 x 2.9cm) strips.

Ⓔ Four 2½ x 1⅛in
(6.2 x 2.9cm) strips.

Ⓕ Four 2½ x 1⅛in
(6.2 x 2.9cm) strips.

Construction

Stripes, see 99
Nine-patch, see 51

Mix and match

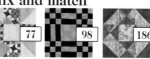
77   98   186

95 Ohio Star

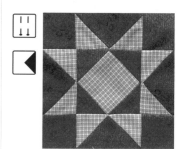

Cut the following

Ⓐ Ⓑ

Ⓐ Four 2in (5cm) squares.

Ⓐ One 4⅛in (10.4cm) square
cut into quarters diagonally to
give four triangles.

Ⓐ Two 2⅜in (5.8cm) squares
cut in half diagonally to give
four triangles.

Ⓑ Four 2⅜in (5.8cm) squares
cut in half diagonally to give
eight triangles.

Ⓑ One 2⅝in (6.5cm) square.

Construction

Diamond in the Square, see 86
Dutchman's Puzzle, see 75
Nine-patch, see 51

Mix and match

40   47   103

96 Classic Curves

Cut the following

Ⓐ One piece using template 96a.
Ⓑ One piece using template 96b.
Ⓒ One piece using template 96b.
Ⓓ One piece using template 96b.
Ⓔ One piece using template 96c.

Construction

 Join the template 96b sections together.

Drunkard's Path, see 122

97 Anvil

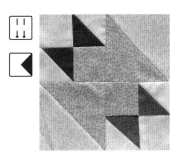

Cut the following

Ⓐ One 3⅞in (9.5cm) square cut in half diagonally to give two triangles.
Ⓑ One 3⅞in (9.5cm) square cut in half diagonally to give two triangles.
Ⓑ Two 2in (5cm) squares.
Ⓒ Two 2in (5cm) squares.
Ⓒ Two 2⅜in (5.8cm) squares cut in half diagonally to give four triangles.
Ⓓ Two 2⅜in (5.8cm) squares cut in half diagonally to give four triangles.

Construction

Half-square Triangles, see 27
Four-patch, see 13

98 Building Blocks

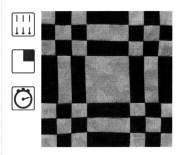

Cut the following

Ⓐ Sixteen 1⅛in (2.9cm) squares.
Ⓐ Eight 2½ x 1⅛in (6.2 x 2.9cm) strips.
Ⓑ One 2½in (6.2cm) square.
Ⓑ Twenty 1⅛in (2.9cm) squares.
Ⓑ Four 2½ x 1⅛in (6.2 x 2.9cm) strips.

Construction

Stripes, see 99
Nine-patch, see 51

Mix and match

 54 58 180

Mix and match

 13 40 75

Mix and match

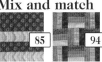 85 94 160

CONSTRUCTION GUIDELINES

99 Stripes

Cut the following

(A) Two 6½ x 2in
(16.2 x 5cm) strips.
(B) Two 6½ x 2in
(16.2 x 5cm) strips.

Quick tip

If you are making several blocks, cut longer strips, sew them together along their entire length and then cut into 6½in (16.2cm) segments.

Construction

Lay the first two strips right sides together and sew along one long edge. Open out and press.

Place the third strip on top of the second, right sides together and with outer edges even. Sew and then press open. Repeat to add the final strip.

Mix and match

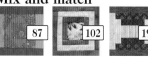

---

100 Sashed Four-patch

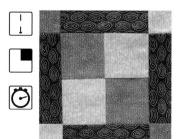

Cut the following

(A) Four 4½ x 1⅛in
(11.2 x 3.7cm) strips.
(B) Two 2⅜in (6.2cm) squares.
(B) Two 1⅛in (3.7cm) squares.
(C) Two 2⅜in (6.2cm) squares.
(C) Two 1⅛in (3.7cm) squares.

Construction

Four-patch, see 13
Nine-patch, see 51

Mix and match

---

101 Long Checks

Cut the following

(A) One 6½ x 2½in
(16.2 x 6.2cm) strip.
(A) Five 2½ x 1¾in
(6.2 x 4.2cm) strips.
(B) Five 2½ x 1¾in
(6.2 x 4.2cm) strips.

Construction

Stripes, see 99

Mix and match

102 White House Steps

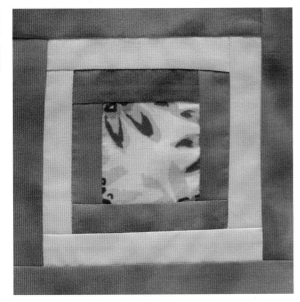

Cut the following

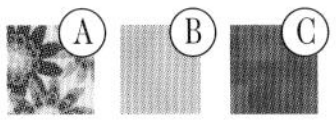

Ⓐ One 2½in (6.2cm) square.

Ⓑ One 3⅞ x 1⅛in
(9.5 x 2.9cm) strip.

Ⓑ Two 4½ x 1⅛in
(11.2 x 2.9cm) strips.

Ⓑ One 5⅛ x 1⅛in
(12.9 x 2.9cm) strip.

Ⓒ One 2½ x 1⅛in
(6.2 x 2.9cm) strip.

Ⓒ Two 3⅛ x 1⅛in
(7.7 x 2.9cm) strips.

Ⓒ One 3⅞ x 1⅛in
(9.5 x 2.9cm) strip.

Ⓒ One 5⅛ x 1⅛in
(12.9 x 2.9cm) strip.

Ⓒ Two 5⅞ x 1⅛in
(14.5 x 2.9cm) strips.

Ⓒ One 6½ x 1⅛in
(16.2 x 2.9cm) strip.

Construction

Log Cabin, see 159

---

103 Three-patch Quilt

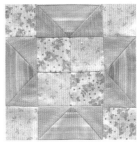

Cut the following

 Ⓐ Ⓑ Ⓒ Ⓓ

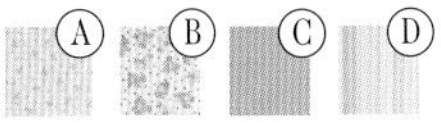

Ⓐ Four 2in (5cm) squares.

Ⓑ Four 2in (5cm) squares.

Ⓒ Four 2⅜in (5.8cm) squares
cut in half diagonally to give
eight triangles.

Ⓓ One 4⅛in (10.4cm) square
cut into quarters diagonally to
give four triangles.

Construction

Dutchman's Puzzle, see 75
Four-patch, see 13
Nine-patch, see 51

Mix and match

37   80   143

---

104 Box in a Box

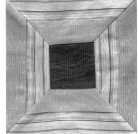

Cut the following

 Ⓐ Ⓑ Ⓒ

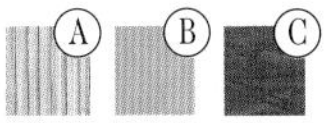

Ⓐ Two 5¼ x 1½in strips
(13.1 x 3.7cm); trim both ends
at a 45-degree angle.

Ⓐ Two 7¼ x 1½in (17.9 x 3.7cm)
strips; trim both ends at a
45-degree angle.

Ⓑ Two 5¼ x 1½in (13.1 x 3.7cm)
strips; trim both ends at a
45-degree angle.

Ⓑ Two 7¼ x 1½in (17.9 x 3.7cm)
strips; trim both ends at a
45-degree angle.

Ⓒ One 2½in (6.2cm) square.

Construction

Stripes, see 99
Spool, see 45

Mix and match

39   171   195

Mix and match

37   80   143

105 Flying X

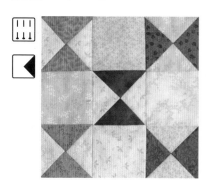

Cut the following

Ⓐ One 2½in (6.2cm) square.

Ⓐ One 3¼in (8cm) square cut into quarters diagonally to give four triangles.

Ⓑ One 2½in (6.2cm) square.

Ⓑ One 3¼in (8cm) square cut into quarters diagonally to give four triangles; you need two of them.

Ⓒ One 2½in (6.2cm) square.

Ⓒ One 3¼in (8cm) square cut into quarters diagonally to give four triangles; you need two of them.

Ⓓ One 2½in (6.2cm) square.

Ⓓ One 3¼in (8cm) square cut into quarters diagonally to give four triangles; you need two of them.

Ⓔ One 3¼in (8cm) square cut into quarters diagonally to give four triangles; you need two of them.

Ⓕ One 3¼in (8cm) square cut into quarters diagonally to give four triangles; you need two of them.

Ⓖ One 3¼in (8cm) square cut into quarters diagonally to give four triangles; you need two of them.

Ⓗ One 3¼in (8cm) square cut into quarters diagonally to give four triangles; you need two of them.

Ⓘ One 3¼in (8cm) square cut into quarters diagonally to give four triangles; you need two of them.

Construction

Four X, see 63

Nine-patch, see 51

Mix and match

62   107   115

106 Simple Flower

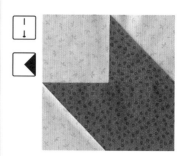

Cut the following

Ⓐ One 3½in (8.7cm) square.

Ⓐ One 3⅞in (9.5cm) square cut in half diagonally to give two triangles.

Ⓑ One 3⅞in (9.5cm) square cut in half diagonally to give two triangles; you need one of them.

Ⓑ One 6⅞ x 3½in (17 x 8.7cm) strip; trim one end at a 45-degree angle.

Construction

Half-square Triangles, see 27

Four-patch, see 13

Mix and match

2   25   28

107 Chain and Hourglass

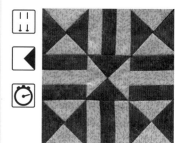

Cut the following

Ⓐ Three 3¼in (8cm) squares cut into quarters diagonally to give twelve triangles; you need ten of them.

Ⓐ Six 2½ x 1⅛in (6.2 x 2.9cm) strips.

Ⓑ Three 3¼in (8cm) squares cut into quarters diagonally to give twelve triangles; you need ten of them.

Ⓑ Six 2½ x 1⅛in (6.2 x 2.9cm) strips.

Construction

Four X, see 63

Stripes, see 99

Nine-patch, see 51

Mix and match

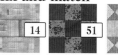

14   51   105

108 Card Trick

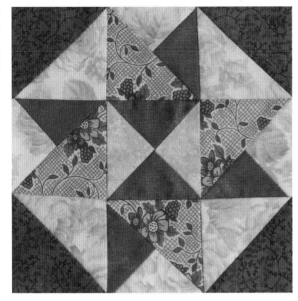

Cut the following

(A) Two 2⅞in (7.2cm) squares cut in half diagonally to give four triangles.

(B) Two 2⅞in (7.2cm) squares cut in half diagonally to give four triangles.

(C) Two 2⅞in (7.2cm) squares cut in half diagonally to give four triangles.

(C) One 3¼in (8cm) square cut into quarters diagonally to give four triangles.

(D) One 3¼in (8cm) square cut into quarters diagonally to give four triangles; you need two of them.

(E) Two 3¼in (8cm) squares cut into quarters diagonally to give eight triangles; you need six of them.

Construction

Half-square Triangles, see 27
Four X, see 63
Nine-patch, see 51

Mix and match

61   105   115

109 Propeller

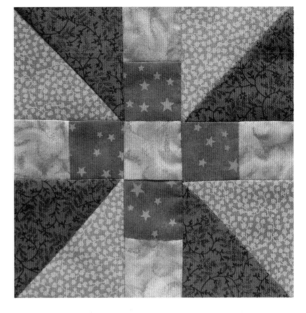

Cut the following

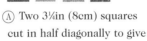

(A) Two 3¼in (8cm) squares cut in half diagonally to give four triangles.

(B) Two 3¼in (8cm) squares cut in half diagonally to give four triangles.

(C) Five 1¾in (4.2cm) squares.

(D) Four 1¾in (4.2cm) squares.

Construction

Join four pairs of squares together.

Half-square Triangles, see 27

Nine-patch, see 51

Mix and match

16   131   156

CONSTRUCTION GUIDELINES

110 Bird in the Air

Cut the following

Ⓐ Two 3⅞in (9.5cm) squares cut in half diagonally to give four triangles; you need three of them.

Ⓑ One 3⅞in (9.5cm) square cut in half diagonally to give two triangles; you need one of them.

Ⓑ One 6⅞in (17cm) square cut in half diagonally to give two triangles; you need one of them.

Construction

 Join a pair alternate coloured small triangles together to make a half-square triangle unit (see block 27).

 Add the remaining small triangles to the sides.

With the pieced unit on top, sew the pieced and large triangles together, adjusting the seam allowance if necessary to create a good point at the centre of the block.

Mix and match

 22 27 164

111 Old Windmill

Cut the following

Ⓐ Two 3¾in (9.5cm) squares cut in half diagonally to give four triangles.

Ⓑ One 4¼in (10.4cm) square cut into quarters diagonally to give four triangles.

Ⓒ One 4¼in (10.4cm) square cut into quarters diagonally to give four triangles.

Construction

Four X, see 63

Half-square Triangles, see 27

Four-patch, see 13

Mix and match

 3 21 114

112 Sam's Favourite

Cut the following

Ⓐ One 3¼in (8.3cm) square cut in half diagonally to give two triangles.

Ⓐ Two 5½ x 1½in (13.7 x 3.7cm) strips.

Ⓑ One 3in (7.6cm) square.

Ⓑ One 1½in (3.7cm) square.

Ⓑ One 5¾in (14.5cm) square cut in half diagonally to give two triangles; you need one of them.

Construction

Bird in the Air, see 110

Four-patch, see 13

Mix and match

 129 166 187

113 Four Squares

Cut the following

Ⓐ Eight 1¼in (3.1cm) squares.
Ⓑ Twelve 1¼in (3.1cm) squares.
Ⓒ Four 1¼in (3.1cm) squares.
Ⓓ Two 2in (5cm) squares.
Ⓓ Four 2 x 1¼in
 (5 x 3.1cm) strips.
Ⓔ Two 2in (5cm) squares.
Ⓕ Two 2in (5cm) squares.
Ⓕ Four 2 x 1¼in
 (5 x 3.1cm) strips.

Construction

Four-patch, see 13
Nine-patch, see 51

114 Flock of Geese

Cut the following

Ⓐ One 3⅞in (9.5cm) square cut in half diagonally to give two triangles.
Ⓑ One 3⅞in (9.5cm) square cut in half diagonally to give two triangles.
Ⓒ Four 2⅜in (5.8cm) squares cut in half diagonally to give eight triangles.
Ⓓ Four 2⅜in (5.8cm) squares cut in half diagonally to give eight triangles.

Construction

Half-square Triangles, see 27
Four-patch, see 13

115 Texas Star

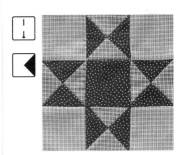

Cut the following

Ⓐ Two 3¼in (8cm) squares cut into quarters diagonally to give eight triangles.
Ⓑ One 2½in (6.2cm) square.
Ⓑ Two 3¼in (8cm) squares cut into quarters diagonally to give eight triangles.
Ⓒ Four 2½in (6.2cm) squares.

Construction

Four X, see 63
Nine-patch, see 51

Mix and match

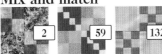 2 59 132

 4 10 93

 43 67 169

116 Grandmother's Choice Variation

Cut the following

Ⓐ Two 4½ x 2½in
(11.2 x 6.2cm) strips.

Ⓑ Two 2⅞in (7.2cm) squares
cut in half diagonally to give
four triangles.

Ⓒ Two 2⅞in (7.2cm) squares
cut in half diagonally to give
four triangles.

Ⓓ One 2½in (6.2cm) square.

Construction

Half-square Triangles, see 27
Four-patch, see 13

Mix and match

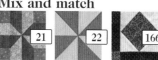

117 Kitty Corner

Cut the following

Ⓐ One 2½in (6.2cm) square.

Ⓐ Four 2½ x 1½in
(6.2 x 3.7cm) strips.

Ⓑ Two 1⅞in (4.7cm) squares
cut in half diagonally to give
four triangles.

Ⓑ Two 2½ x 1½in
(6.2 x 3.7cm) strips.

Ⓒ Four 1⅞in (4.7cm) squares.

Ⓒ Two 2½ x 1½in
(6.2 x 3.7cm) strips.

Ⓓ Six 1⅞in (4.7cm) squares
cut in half diagonally to give
twelve triangles.

Construction

Diamond in the Square, see 86
Stripes, see 99
Nine-patch, see 51

Mix and match

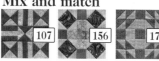

118 Around the Bend

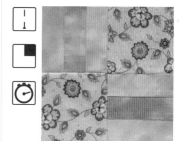

Cut the following

Ⓐ Two 3½ x 1½in
(8.7 x 3.7cm) strips.

Ⓑ Two 3½ x 1½in
(8.7 x 3.7cm) strips.

Ⓒ Two 3½ x 1½in
(8.7 x 3.7cm) strips.

Ⓓ Two 3½in (8.7cm) squares.

Construction

Stripes, see 99
Four-patch, see 13

Mix and match

119 Mitred Corner

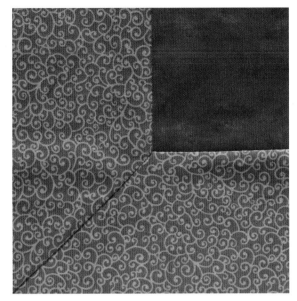

Cut the following

Ⓐ One 3½in (8.7cm) square.
Ⓑ Two 6¾ x 3½in (17 x 8.7cm) strips; trim one end at a 45-degree angle.

Construction

Sew one angled strip to the square, stopping ¼in (6mm) from the edge of the square at the inner angle.
Sew the remaining strip to the adjacent side of the square in the same way, again stopping ¼in (6mm) from the edge. Fold the square in half diagonally, right sides together, so that the angled edges of the strips meet. Starting at the exact position where you stopped sewing previously, join the remaining seam (see page 113).

Quick tip

If your fabric is directional, check before you trim the angles to ensure that the fabric pattern will meet in the desired way at the mitred corner.

Mix and match

120 Summer Sky

Cut the following

Ⓐ One 7¼in (17.9cm) square cut into quarters diagonally to give four triangles; you need one of them.
Ⓑ One 7¼in (17.9cm) square cut into quarters diagonally to give four triangles; you need one of them.
Ⓑ One 6⅞in (17cm) square cut in half diagonally to give two triangles; you need one of them.

Construction

Four X, see 63
Half-square Triangles, see 27

Mix and match

121 Tam's Patch

Cut the following

Ⓐ Two 3½ x 2in (8.7 x 5cm) strips.
Ⓐ Two 2in (5cm) squares.
Ⓑ Two 2in (5cm) squares.
Ⓒ Two 3½in (8.7cm) squares.

Construction

Four-patch, see 13

Mix and match

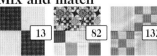

CONSTRUCTION GUIDELINES

122 Drunkard's Path

Cut the following

Ⓐ One piece using template 122a.
Ⓑ One piece using template 122b.

Construction

Fold each piece in half and mark the centre points of the curved edges with a small crease.

Open out the pieces and, with curved edges aligned and piece 122a on top, match and pin the midpoint creases. Pin the two side edges to stop them from distorting. Slowly sew the seam, removing the pins as you come to them. Do not clip the seam allowance.

Mix and match

123 Cotton Reel

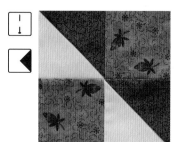

Cut the following

Ⓐ Two 3½in (8.7cm) squares.
Ⓑ One 3⅞in (9.5cm) square cut in half diagonally to give two triangles.
Ⓒ One 3⅞in (9.5cm) square cut in half diagonally to give two triangles.

Construction

Half-square Triangles, see 27
Four-patch, see 13

Mix and match

124 Triangles

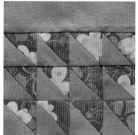

Cut the following

Ⓐ Six 2⅜in (5.8cm) squares cut in half diagonally to give twelve triangles.
Ⓐ One 6½in x 2in (16.2 x 5cm) strip.
Ⓑ Six 2⅜in (5.8cm) squares cut in half diagonally to give twelve triangles.

Construction

Half-square Triangles, see 27
Stripes, see 99

Mix and match

82   114   137

125 Memory

Cut the following

Ⓐ One 2½in (6.2cm) square.

Ⓐ Four 1⅞in (4.7cm) squares cut in half diagonally to give eight triangles.

Ⓑ Four 1½in (3.7cm) squares.

Ⓑ Eight 1⅞in (4.7cm) squares cut in half diagonally to give sixteen triangles.

Ⓑ One 3¼in (8cm) square cut into quarters diagonally to give four triangles.

Ⓒ Four 1½in (3.7cm) squares.

Ⓒ Four 1⅞in (4.7cm) squares cut in half diagonally to give eight triangles.

Ⓒ One 3¼in (8cm) square cut into quarters diagonally to give four triangles.

Construction

Dutchman's Puzzle, see 75
Half-square Triangles, see 27
Four-patch, see 13
Nine-patch, see 51

Mix and match

40   47   108

126 Buzzard's Roost

Cut the following

Ⓐ Ⓑ Ⓒ Ⓓ

Ⓐ Two 2⅜in (5.8cm) squares cut in half diagonally to give four triangles.

Ⓐ Two 3½ x 2in (8.7 x 5cm) strips.

Ⓑ Four 2in (5cm) squares.

Ⓑ One 3½in (8.7cm) square.

Ⓒ Two 3½ x 2in (8.7 x 5cm) strips.

Ⓓ Two 2⅜in (5.8cm) squares cut in half diagonally to give four triangles.

Ⓓ Four 2in (5cm) squares.

Construction

Fast Geese, see 134
Half-square Triangles, see 27
Nine-patch, see 51

Mix and match

95   100   188

127 Wide Stripe

Cut the following

Ⓐ Ⓑ

Ⓐ One 6½in x 4⅜in (16.2 x 11.2cm) strip.

Ⓑ One 6½ x 2½in (16.2 x 6.2cm) strip.

Construction

Stripes, see 99

Mix and match

99   138   187

128 The House That Jack Built

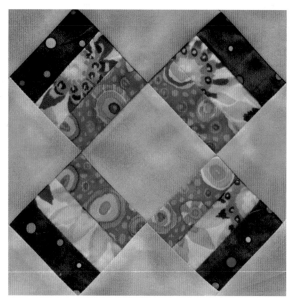

Cut the following

(A) Four 2⅝ x 1¼in
(6.5 x 3.1cm) strips.
(B) Four 2⅝ x 1¼in
(6.5 x 3.1cm) strips.
(C) Four 2⅝ x 1¼in
(6.5 x 3.1cm) strips.
(D) One 4¼in (10.4cm) square
cut into quarters diagonally to
give four triangles.
(D) Two 2⅜in (5.8cm) squares
cut in half diagonally to give
four triangles.
(D) One 2⅝in (6.5cm) square.

Construction

Stripes, see 99
Mosaic, see 147

Mix and match

 50
 147
 173

---

129 Twelve Triangles

Cut the following

A Two 2⅜in (5.8cm) squares
cut in half diagonally to give
four triangles.
B One 4¼in (10.4cm) square
cut into quarters diagonally to
give four triangles.
C One 2⅝in (6.5cm) square.
C Two 3⅞in (9.5cm) squares
cut in half diagonally to give
four triangles.

Construction

Diamond in the Square, see 86

Mix and match

 9
 70
 151

---

130 King's Crown

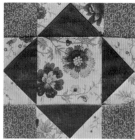

Cut the following

A Four 2in (5cm) squares.
B Four 3½ x 2in
(8.7 x 5cm) strips.
C Eight 2in (5cm) squares.
C One 3½in (8.7cm) square.

Construction

Fast Geese, see 134
Nine-patch, see 51

Mix and match

 30
 103
 155

131 Sister's Choice

Cut the following

 Ⓐ Ⓑ Ⓒ Ⓓ

Ⓐ Four 1⅝in (4.2cm) squares.

Ⓑ Two 2in (5cm) squares cut in half diagonally to give four triangles.

Ⓑ Four 3¼ x 1⅝in (8 x 4.2cm) strips; trim one end at a 45-degree angle.

Ⓒ Four 1⅝in (4.2cm) squares.

Ⓒ Four 2in (5cm) squares cut in half diagonally to give eight triangles.

Ⓓ Five 1⅝in (4.2cm) squares.

Construction

 Half-square Triangles, see 27

 Sew a triangle to each angled strip.

 Four-patch, see 13

Sew five squares together to form the horizontal centre strip.

 Sew the remaining squares together in pairs.

Join the units to form the top and bottom rows.
Join the rows to complete the block.

Mix and match

 16   162   172

132 Four- and Nine-patch

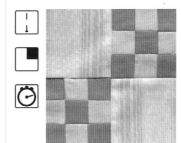

Cut the following

Ⓐ Ⓑ Ⓒ

Ⓐ Ten 1½in (3.7cm) squares.

Ⓑ Eight 1½in (3.7cm) squares.

Ⓒ Two 3½in (8.7cm) squares.

Construction

Nine-patch, see 51
Four-patch, see 13

Mix and match

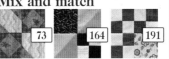 73 164 191

133 Diamond Border

Cut the following

Ⓐ Ⓑ Ⓒ

Ⓐ Two 2⅜in (5.8cm) squares cut in half diagonally to give four triangles.

Ⓑ Two 2⅜in (5.8cm) squares cut in half diagonally to give four triangles.

Ⓒ Four 2⅜in (5.8cm) squares cut in half diagonally to give eight triangles.

Ⓒ One 6½ x 3½in (16.2 x 8.7cm) strip.

Construction

Half-square Triangles, see 27
Four-patch, see 13

Mix and match

 130   135   137

CONSTRUCTION GUIDELINES

134 Fast Geese

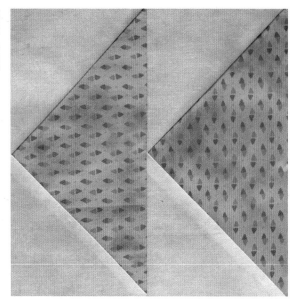

Cut the following

Ⓐ Two 6½ x 3½in
(16.2 x 8.7cm) strips.
Ⓑ Four 3½in (8.7cm) squares.

Construction

 Lay a square face down on one end of a strip with the edges level. Sew diagonally across the square from point to point. To make it easier, draw the sewing line with pencil first. Press open and cut away the excess fabric from the back of the square. Repeat to add a square at the other end of the strip.

Make a second unit in the same way and join the two together.

Quick tip

When sewing the squares to the strips, sew a second line of stitching ½in (1.2cm) away from the first before cutting away the excess fabric between the two lines of stitching. This will create a readymade half-square triangle unit. Beware: these will sit in your sewing drawer for years to come, nagging at you to make use of them.

Mix and match

 23
 63
 86

135 Zig Zag

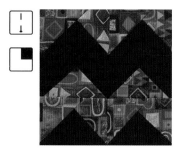

Cut the following

Ⓐ Ⓑ

Ⓐ Two 3½ x 2⅛in
(8.7 x 6.2cm) strips.
Ⓐ Eight 2⅛in (6.2cm) squares.
Ⓑ Four 3½ x 2⅛in
(8.7 x 6.2cm) strips.
Ⓑ Four 2⅛in (6.2cm) squares.

Construction

Fast Geese, see 134
Stripes, see 99

Quick tip

Don't worry: the geese points are meant to be away from the edges of the units.

Mix and match

 126
 137
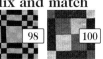 194

136 Sashed Nine-patch

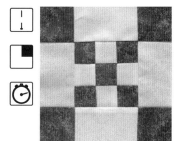

Cut the following

Ⓐ Ⓑ

Ⓐ Four 3½ x 2in
(8.7 x 5cm) strips.
Ⓐ Four 1⅜in (3.7cm) squares.
Ⓑ Four 2in (5cm) squares.
Ⓑ Five 1⅜in (3.7cm) squares.

Construction

Nine-patch, see 51

Mix and match

98 100
 167

137 Small Triangles and Stripes

Cut the following

Ⓐ Two 2⅜in (5.8cm) squares cut in half diagonally to give four triangles.

Ⓐ One 6½ x 2in (16.2 x 5cm) strip.

Ⓑ Two 2⅜in (5.8cm) squares cut in half diagonally to give four triangles.

Ⓑ Two 6½ x 2in (16.2 x 5cm) strips.

Construction

Half-square Triangles, see 27
Stripes, see 99

.

Mix and match

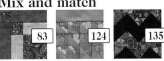

138 Large Triangles and Stripes

Cut the following

Ⓐ One 6½ x 2⅓in (16.2 x 6.2cm) strip.

Ⓑ One 6½ x 2⅓in (16.2 x 6.2cm) strip.

Ⓑ Two 2⅞in (7.2cm) squares cut in half diagonally to give four triangles; you need three of them.

Ⓒ Two 2⅞in (7.2cm) squares cut in half diagonally to give four triangles; you need three of them.

Construction

Half-square Triangles, see 27
Stripes, see 99

Mix and match

139 Yankee Puzzle I

Cut the following

(A) Eight 2⅜in (5.8cm) squares cut in half diagonally to give sixteen triangles.
(B) Eight 2⅜in (5.8cm) squares cut in half diagonally to give sixteen triangles.

Construction
Half-square Triangles, see 27
Four-patch, see 13

Mix and match

140 Triangle Tiles

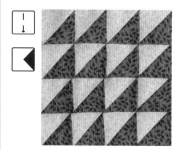

Cut the following

Mix and match

141 Colorado Quilt

Cut the following

Mix and match

142 Whirlpool

Cut the following

Mix and match

143 Pieced Star

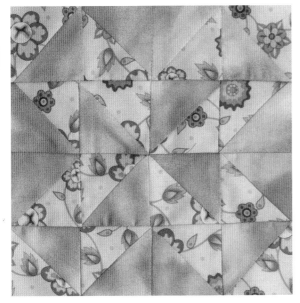

Cut the following

 (A) (B)

Mix and match

 40   103   168

144 Yankee Puzzle II

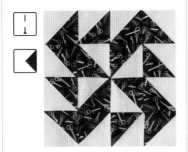

Cut the following

 (A) (B)

Mix and match

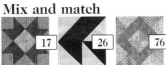 17   26   76

145 Hopscotch

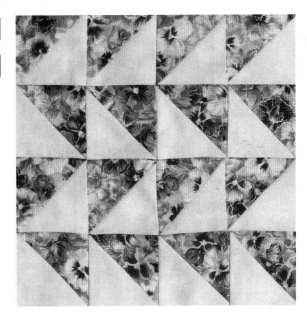

Cut the following

(A) (B)

Mix and match

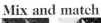 23   24   103

146 Fly foot

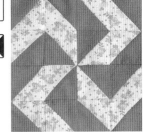

Cut the following

(A) (B)

Mix and match

 8   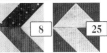 25   75

CONSTRUCTION GUIDELINES

147 Mosaic

Cut the following

Ⓐ One 2⅝in (6.5cm) square.

Ⓑ One 2⅝in (6.5cm) square.

Ⓒ One 2⅝in (6.5cm) square.

Ⓓ One 2⅝in (6.5cm) square.

Ⓔ One 2⅝in (6.5cm) square.

Ⓔ One 2¼in (5.8cm) square cut in half diagonally to give two triangles.

Ⓕ One 4⅛in (10.4cm) square cut into quarters diagonally to give four triangles; you need two of them.

Ⓕ One 2¼in (5.8cm) square cut in half diagonally to give two triangles.

Ⓖ One 4⅛in (10.4cm) square cut into quarters diagonally to give four triangles; you need two of them.

 Add a small triangle to another side of the square to create a triangular pieced unit.

 Repeat this process to make a second triangular unit.

 Sew the remaining squares together in a row, then add a small triangle at each end to form the central diagonal strip. Join the three sections together.

Construction

 Sew two large triangles to opposite sides of a square.

Mix and match

 1   128   188

---

148 Picket

Cut the following

 Ⓐ   Ⓑ

Ⓐ Two 3½ x 2in (8.7 x 5cm) strips.

Ⓑ Two 3½ x 2in (8.7 x 5cm) strips.

Ⓑ One 6½ x 3½in (16.2 x 8.7cm) strip.

Construction

Stripes, see 99

Mix and match

 13   99   137

---

149 Small-centre Nine-patch

Cut the following

 Ⓐ Ⓑ

Ⓐ Four 3in (7.6cm) squares.

Ⓐ One 1½in (3.7cm) square.

Ⓑ Four 3 x 1½in (7.6 x 3.7cm) strips.

Construction

Nine-patch, see 51

Mix and match

158 160 172

150 Wild Goose Chase

Cut the following

Ⓐ Two 2in (5cm) squares cut in half diagonally to give four triangles.

Ⓑ One 2in (5cm) square cut in half diagonally to give two triangles.

Ⓑ One 3¼in (8cm) square cut in half diagonally to give two triangles.

Ⓒ Four 2in (5cm) squares cut in half diagonally to give eight triangles.

Ⓒ Four 2⅞ x 1⅝in (7.2 x 4.2cm) strips.

Ⓓ One 1⅝in (4.2cm) square.

Ⓓ One 2in (5cm) square cut in half diagonally to give two triangles.

Ⓓ One 3¼in (8cm) square cut in half diagonally to give two triangles.

Construction
Bird in the Air, see 110
Nine-patch, see 51

151 Flying Geese Variation

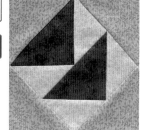

Cut the following

Ⓐ Two 3⅞in (9.5cm) squares cut in half diagonally to give four triangles.

Ⓑ Two 4¾ x 2⅝in (11.8 x 6.5cm) strips.

Ⓒ Four 2⅝in (6.5cm) squares.

Construction
Fast Geese, see 134
Diamond in the Square, see 86

152 Air Castle

Cut the following

Ⓐ Four 2⅞in (7.2cm) squares cut in half diagonally to give eight triangles.

Ⓐ One 3¼in (8cm) square cut into quarters diagonally to give four triangles.

Ⓐ One 1⅞in (4.7cm) square.

Ⓑ Two 2⅞in (7.2cm) squares cut in half diagonally to give four triangles.

Ⓑ One 3¼in (8cm) square cut into quarters diagonally to give four triangles.

Ⓑ Two 1⅞in (4.7cm) squares cut in half diagonally to give four triangles.

Construction
Four X, see 63
Half-square Triangles, see 27
Diamond in the Square, see 86
Nine-patch, see 51

Mix and match
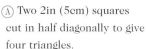 6 160 177

Mix and match
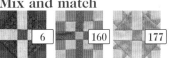 70 129 130

Mix and match
 17 115 169

153 Nine-patch Variation

Cut the following

(A) One 2⅞in (7.2cm) square cut in half diagonally to give two triangles; you need one of them.

(A) One 2½in (6.2cm) square.

(B) One 2⅞in (7.2cm) square cut in half diagonally to give two triangles; you need one of them.

(B) One 2½in (6.2cm) square.

(C) One 2⅞in (7.2cm) square cut in half diagonally to give two triangles; you need one of them.

(C) One 2½in (6.2cm) square.

(D) One 2⅞in (7.2cm) square cut in half diagonally to give two triangles; you need one of them.

(E) One 2⅞in (7.2cm) square cut in half diagonally to give two triangles; you need one of them.

(E) One 2½in (6.2cm) square.

(F) One 2⅞in (7.2cm) square cut in half diagonally to give two triangles; you need one of them.

(F) One 2½in (6.2cm) square.

(G) One 2½in (6.2cm) square.

Construction

Half-square Triangles, see 27

Nine-patch, see 51

Mix and match

23   27   159

154 Goose Stripe

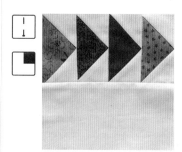

Cut the following

(A) One 6½ x 3½in (16.2 x 8.7cm) strip.

(A) Eight 2in (5cm) squares.

(B) One 3½ x 2in (8.7 x 5cm) strip.

(C) One 3½ x 2in (8.7 x 5cm) strip.

(D) One 3½ x 2in (8.7 x 5cm) strip.

(E) One 3½ x 2in (8.7 x 5cm) strip.

Construction

Fast Geese, see 134

Stripes, see 99

Mix and match

151   170   194

155 Album Quilt

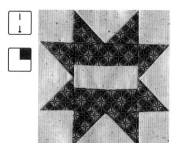

Cut the following

(A) Eight 2in (5cm) squares.

(A) Two 3½ x 1½in (8.7 x 3.7cm) strips.

(B) Four 2in (5cm) squares.

(B) Four 3½ x 2in (8.7 x 5cm) strips.

(B) One 3½ x 1½in (8.7 x 3.7cm) strip.

Construction

Stripes, see 99

Fast Geese, see 134

Nine-patch, see 51

Mix and match

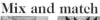

103   125   168

156 Garden of Eden

Cut the following

(A) One 1¾in (4.2cm) square.
(B) Four 1¾in (4.2cm) squares.
(C) Two 2in (5cm) squares cut in half diagonally to give four triangles.
(D) Four 1¾in (4.2cm) squares.
(E) Six 2in (5cm) squares cut in half diagonally to give twelve triangles.
(F) Four 2⅛in (5.6cm) squares.

Construction

Join four pairs of small squares together.

Diamond in the square, see 86
Nine-patch, see 51

157 Endless Stair

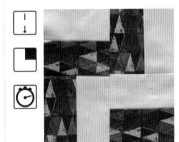

Cut the following

(A) Four 3½ x 2in (8.7 x 5cm) strips.
(B) Four 3½ x 2in (8.7 x 5cm) strips

Construction

Stripes, see 99
Four-patch, see 13

158 Duck's Foot

Cut the following

(A) Five 1¾in (4.2cm) squares.
(B) Four 2⅛in (5.4cm) squares cut in half diagonally to give eight triangles.
(C) Two 3¼in (8cm) squares cut in half diagonally to give four triangles.
(D) Four 2⅞ x 1¾in (7.2 x 4.2cm) strips.

Construction

Bird in the Air, see 110
Nine-patch, see 51

Mix and match

109 117 177

Mix and match

13 127 138

Mix and match

16 109 162

CONSTRUCTION GUIDELINES

159 Log Cabin

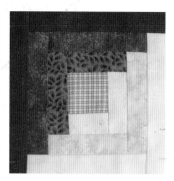

Cut the following

Ⓐ One 2in (5cm) square.

Ⓑ One 2 x 1¼in
(5 x 3.1cm) strip.

Ⓑ One 2¾ x 1¼in
(6.8 x 3.1cm) strip.

Ⓒ One 2¾ x 1¼in
(6.8 x 3.1cm) strip.

Ⓒ One 3½ x 1¼in
(8.7 x 3.1cm) strip.

Ⓓ One 3½ x 1¼in
(8.7 x 3.1cm) strip.

Ⓓ One 4¼ x 1¼in
(10.4 x 3.1cm) strip.

Ⓔ One 4¼ x 1¼in
(10.4 x 3.1cm) strip.

Ⓔ One 5 x 1¼in
(12.4 x 3.1cm) strip.

Ⓕ One 5 x 1¼in
(12.4 x 3.1cm) strip.

Ⓕ One 5¾ x 1¼in
(14.3 x 3.1cm) strip.

Ⓖ One 5¾ x 1¼in
(14.3 x 3.1cm) strip.

Ⓖ One 6½ x 1¼in
(16.2 x 3.1cm) strip.

Construction

Sew the shortest
strip to one side
of the centre square.

Add a matching
coloured strip to
the square and
the end of the first strip.

Repeat this process
to add the next two
coloured strips.
Continue adding strips in this
way, making sure that you
maintain the light/dark balance.

Mix and match

 19   153   180

---

160 Crossed Squares

Cut the following

Ⓐ Eight 1¾in (4.2cm) squares.

Ⓑ Eight 1¾in (4.2cm) squares.

Ⓒ One 1½in (3.7cm) square.

Ⓓ Four 3 x 1½in
(7.6 x 3.7cm) strips.

Construction

Four-patch, see 13

Nine-patch, see 51

Mix and match

 16   131   149

---

161 Inverted V

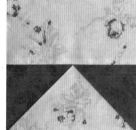

Cut the following

Ⓐ Two 6½ x 3½in
(16.2 x 8.7cm) strips.

Ⓑ Two 3½in (8.7cm) squares.

Construction

Fast Geese, see 134

Stripes, see 99

Mix and match

 120   123   134

162 Five-patch Star

Cut the following

Ⓐ Eight 1¾in (4.2cm) squares.

Ⓐ Four 2in (5cm) squares cut in half diagonally to give eight triangles.

Ⓑ Four 2in (5cm) squares cut in half diagonally to give eight triangles.

Ⓒ Five 1¾in (4.2cm) squares.

Ⓓ Four 1¾in (4.2cm) squares.

Construction

 Half-square Triangles, see 27

 Four-patch, see 13

Sew five squares together to form the horizontal centre strip.

Sew the remaining squares together in pairs.

Join the units to form the top and bottom rows. Join the rows to complete the block.

163 Railroad

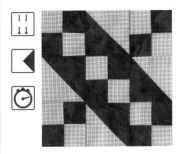

Cut the following

Ⓐ Ten 1½in (3.7cm) squares.

Ⓐ Two 2⅞in (7.2cm) squares cut in half diagonally to give four triangles.

Ⓑ Ten 1½in (3.7cm) squares.

Ⓑ Two 2⅞in (7.2cm) squares cut in half diagonally to give four triangles.

Construction

Four-patch, see 13
Half-square Triangles, see 27
Nine-patch, see 51

164 Cotton Reel Variation

Cut the following

Ⓐ One 3½in (8.7cm) square.

Ⓑ One 3⅞in (9.5cm) square cut in half diagonally to give two triangles.

Ⓒ One 3⅞in (9.5cm) square cut in half diagonally to give two triangles.

Ⓓ Two 2in (5cm) squares.

Ⓔ Two 2in (5cm) squares.

Construction

Half-square Triangles, see 27
Four-patch, see 13

Mix and match

158 167 179

Mix and match

50 59 81

Mix and match

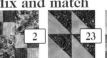
2 23 132

165 Star X

Cut the following

Ⓐ Two 2⅞in (7.2cm) squares cut in half diagonally to give four triangles.

Ⓐ One 3¼in (8cm) square cut into quarters diagonally to give four triangles; you need two of them.

Ⓑ Two 2⅞in (7.2cm) squares cut in half diagonally to give four triangles.

Ⓒ Three 3¼in (8cm) squares cut into quarters diagonally to give twelve triangles; you need ten of them.

Ⓓ Two 3¼in (8cm) squares cut into quarters diagonally to give eight triangles.

Construction

Half-square Triangles, see 27

Four X, see 63

Nine-patch, see 51

Mix and match

44 61 147

166 Half-sashed Diamond

Cut the following

Ⓐ One 4in (10cm) square.

Ⓐ One 1½in (3.7cm) square.

Ⓑ Two 3¼in (8.3cm) squares cut in half diagonally to give four triangles.

Ⓒ Two 5½ x 1½in (13.7 x 3.7cm) strips.

Construction

Diamond in the Square, see 86

Four-patch, see 13

Mix and match

112 129 130

167 Thrifty

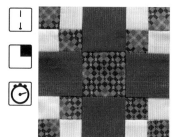

Cut the following

Ⓐ Eight 1½in (3.7cm) squares.

Ⓐ One 2½in (6.2cm) square.

Ⓑ Eight 1½in (3.7cm) squares.

Ⓒ Four 2½in (6.2cm) squares.

Construction

Four-patch, see 13

Nine-patch, see 51

Mix and match

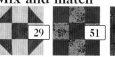

29 51 176

168 Sawtooth Star

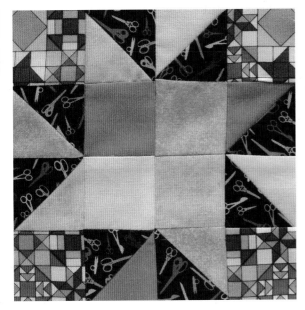

Cut the following

Ⓐ Four 2in (5cm) squares.

Ⓑ One 2in (5cm) square.

Ⓑ One 2⅜in (5.8cm) square cut in half diagonally to give two triangles.

Ⓒ One 2in (5cm) square.

Ⓒ One 2⅜in (5.8cm) square cut in half diagonally to give two triangles.

Ⓓ One 2in (5cm) square.

Ⓓ One 2⅜in (5.8cm) square cut in half diagonally to give two triangles.

Ⓔ One 2in (5cm) square.

Ⓔ One 2⅜in (5.8cm) square cut in half diagonally to give two triangles.

Ⓕ Four 2⅜in (5.8cm) squares cut in half diagonally to give eight triangles.

Construction

Half-square Triangles, see 27

Four-patch, see 13

Mix and match

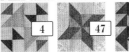
4   47   139

169 Aunt Dinah

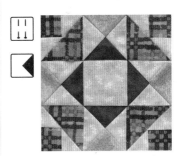

Cut the following

Ⓐ Four 1½in (3.7cm) squares.

Ⓐ Two 2⅞in (7.2cm) squares cut in half diagonally to give four triangles.

Ⓑ Four 1⅞in (4.7cm) squares cut in half diagonally to give eight triangles.

Ⓑ Two 3¼in (8cm) squares cut into quarters diagonally to give eight triangles.

Ⓑ One 2½in (6.2cm) square.

Ⓒ One 3¼in (8cm) square cut into quarters diagonally to give four triangles.

Ⓓ One 3¼in (8cm) square cut into quarters diagonally to give four triangles.

Construction

Bird in the Air, see 110

Four X, see 63

Nine-patch, see 51

Mix and match

105   167   188

170 Corner Sashed Geese

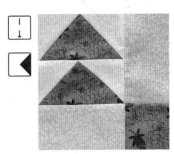

Cut the following

Ⓐ Ⓑ Ⓒ

Ⓐ Four 2½in (6.2cm) squares.

Ⓑ Two 4½ x 2½in (11.2 x 6.2cm) strips.

Ⓒ One 2½in (6.2cm) square.

Ⓒ Two 4½ x 2½in (11.2 x 6.2cm) strips.

Construction

Fast Geese, see 134

Four-patch, see 13

Mix and match

116   187   194

171 Four X Variation

Cut the following

Ⓐ Two 7¼ x 1½in (17.9 x 3.7cm) strips; trim both ends at a 45-degree angle.

Ⓑ Two 7¼ x 1½in (17.9 x 3.7cm) strips; trim both ends at a 45-degree angle.

Ⓒ Two 5¼ x 1½in (13.1 x 3.7cm) strips; trim both ends at a 45-degree angle.

Ⓓ Two 5¼ x 1½in (13.1 x 3.7cm) strips; trim both ends at a 45-degree angle.

Ⓔ One 3⅛in (8cm) square cut into quarters diagonally to give four triangles; you need two of them.

Ⓕ One 3⅛in (8cm) square cut into quarters diagonally to give four triangles; you need two of them.

Construction

 Mark the centre point of each strip with a small crease. Lay pairs in the correct colour combinations right sides together and sew. Open out and press.

 Add the triangles to complete each quarter of the block.

 Sew the short sides of pairs of units together. Join the two sections, making sure the centre points are sharp.

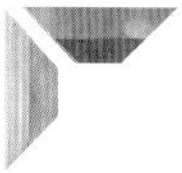

Mix and match

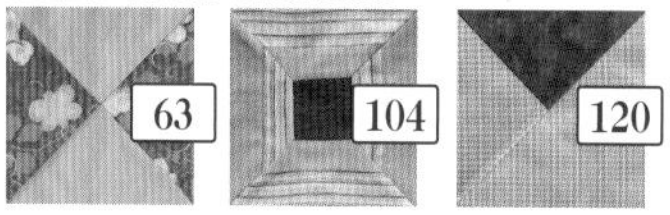

---

172 Red Cross

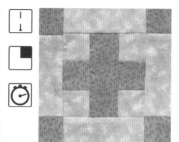

Cut the following

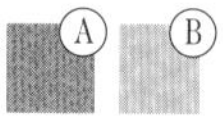

Ⓐ Six 1⅝in (4.2cm) squares.

Ⓐ One 4¼ x 1⅝in (10.4 x 4.2cm) strip.

Ⓑ Four 1⅝in (4.2cm) squares.

Ⓑ Four 4¼ x 1⅝in (10.4 x 4.2cm) strips.

Construction

Nine-patch, see 51

Mix and match

173 Coxey's Army

Cut the following

Ⓐ Six 1⅝in (4.2cm) squares.

Ⓐ Four 4⅛ x 1⅛in (10.2 x 2.9cm) strips.

Ⓑ Two 1⅝in (4.2cm) squares.

Ⓑ Four 4⅛ x 1⅛in (10.2 x 2.9cm) strips.

Ⓒ Two 2⅝in (6.5cm) squares cut in half diagonally to give four triangles.

Construction

Four-patch, see 13

Diamond in the Square, see 86

Stripes, see 99

Nine-patch, see 51

Mix and match

174 Johnny Around the Corner

Cut the following

Ⓐ Two 2in (5cm) squares
cut in half diagonally to give
four triangles.

Ⓐ Nine 1¾in (4.2cm) squares.

Ⓑ Two 2in (5cm) squares
cut in half diagonally to give
four triangles.

Ⓑ Twelve 1¾in (4.2cm) squares.

Construction

Half-square Triangles, see 27
Stripes, see 99

175 Sashed Geese

Cut the following

Ⓐ Two 1½in (3.7cm) squares.

Ⓐ Four 2½in (6.2cm) squares.

Ⓑ Two 1½in (3.7cm) squares.

Ⓑ Two 4½ x 2½in
(11.2 x 6.2cm) strips.

Ⓒ Four 4½ x 1½in
(11.2 x 3.7cm) strips.

Construction

Fast Geese, see 134
Nine-patch, see 51

176 Comfort Quilt

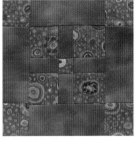

Cut the following

Ⓐ Eight 1⅞in (4.7cm) squares.

Ⓐ One 1⅛in (2.9cm) square.

Ⓑ Four 3¾ x 1⅞in
(9.5 x 4.7cm) strips.

Ⓑ Four 1⅞ x 1⅛in
(4.7 x 2.9cm) strips.

Construction

Nine-patch, see 51

Mix and match

16   162   179

Mix and match

8   154   173

Mix and match

12   130   184

177 Goose Tracks

Cut the following

Ⓐ One 1⅝in (4.2cm) square.

Ⓐ Two 2⅜in (5.8cm) squares cut into quarters diagonally to give eight triangles.

Ⓐ Two 3⅛in (8cm) squares cut in half diagonally to give four triangles.

Ⓑ Four 1⅝in (4.2cm) squares.

Ⓑ Two 2⅜in (5.8cm) squares cut into quarters diagonally to give eight triangles.

Ⓑ Four 2⅞ x 1⅝in (7.2 x 4.2cm) strips.

 Sew a pair of these pieced units to each corner square.

 Fold each large triangle in half and mark the centre of the long edges with a small crease. Sew a pieced triangular unit to each large triangle, aligning the centre points. Nine-patch, see 51

Construction

Sew pairs of small triangles together along their short edges, with their right-angled edges aligned.

178 Forest Paths

Cut the following

Ⓐ Four 1½in (3.7cm) squares.

Ⓐ Two 2⅞in (7.2cm) squares cut in half diagonally to give four triangles.

Ⓑ Two 2⅞in (7.2cm) squares cut in half diagonally to give four triangles.

Ⓒ Four 4½ x 1½in (11.2 x 3.7cm) strips.

Construction

Half-square Triangles, see 27

Four-patch, see 13

Nine-patch, see 51

179 English Wedding Ring

Cut the following

Ⓐ Eight 2in (5cm) squares cut in half diagonally to give sixteen triangles.

Ⓐ Five 1⅝in (4.2cm) squares.

Ⓑ Eight 2in (5cm) squares cut in half diagonally to give sixteen triangles.

Ⓑ Four 1⅝in (4.2cm) squares.

Construction

Half-square Triangles, see 27

Stripes, see 99

Mix and match

Mix and match

Mix and match

180 Off-Centre Log Cabin

Cut the following

Ⓐ One 1½in (3.7cm) square.

Ⓑ Ⓒ Ⓓ Ⓔ 1¼in (3.1cm)
wide strips.

Ⓕ Ⓖ Ⓗ Ⓘ 1in (2.5cm)
wide strips.

Construction

Log Cabin, see 159

181 Philadelphia Pavement

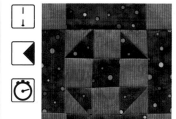

Cut the following

Ⓐ Eight 1¾in (4.2cm) squares.

Ⓐ Two 2in (5cm) squares
cut in half diagonally to give
four triangles.

Ⓑ One 1¾in (4.2cm) square.

Ⓑ Two 2in (5cm) squares
cut in half diagonally to give
four triangles.

Ⓑ Four 4⅛ x 1¾in
(10.2 x 4.2cm) strips.

Construction

Half-square Triangles, see 27
Nine-patch, see 51

182 Plain Block

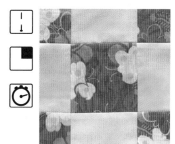

Cut the following

Ⓐ Four 2in (5cm) squares.

Ⓐ One 3½in (8.7cm) square.

Ⓑ Four 3½ x 2in
(8.7 x 5cm) strips.

Construction

Nine-patch, see 51

Mix and match

7   19   153

Mix and match

29   160   184

Mix and match

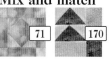

71   170   178

CONSTRUCTION GUIDELINES

183 Starry Night

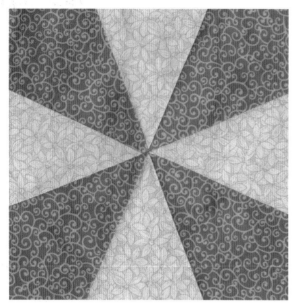

Cut the following

Ⓐ Four pieces using template 183a.

Ⓑ Four pieces using template 183b.

Construction

Join into pairs of alternate colours, matching the edges that will form the sides and corners of the block, not the centre points.

Join the pairs to form each half of the block. Sew the two halves together.

Quick tip

If you are unsure about your accuracy, leave a little extra seam allowance on the sides that will form the edges of the block and trim square when the block is complete.

184 Counterpane Variation

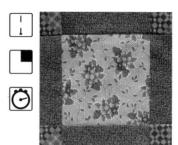

Cut the following

Ⓐ One 4⅜in (11.2cm) square.

Ⓑ Four 4½ x 1⅜in (11.2 x 3.7cm) strips.

Ⓒ Four 1⅜in (3.7cm) squares.

Construction

Nine-patch, see 51

185 Pie Slices

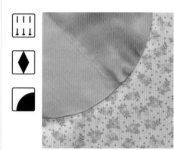

Cut the following

Ⓐ One piece using template 185a.

Ⓑ One piece using template 185b.

Ⓒ One piece using template 185b.

Construction

Sew the template 185b pieces together.

Drunkard's Path, see 122

Mix and match

 1

 51

 69

Mix and match

 87

100

178

Mix and match

 12

54

 96

186 Swamp Angel

Cut the following

Ⓐ Two 3¼in (8cm) squares cut into quarters diagonally to give eight triangles.

Ⓑ Two 3¼in (8cm) squares cut into quarters diagonally to give eight triangles.

Ⓒ Two 2⅞in (7.2cm) squares cut in half diagonally to give four triangles.

Ⓓ Two 2⅞in (7.2cm) squares cut in half diagonally to give four triangles.

Ⓔ One 2½in (6.2cm) square.

Construction

Half-square Triangles, see 27

Four X, see 63

Nine-patch, see 51

187 Rosie's Favourite

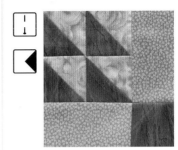

Cut the following

Ⓐ Two 2⅞in (7.2cm) squares cut in half diagonally to give four triangles.

Ⓐ One 2½in (6.2cm) square.

Ⓑ Two 2⅞in (7.2cm) squares cut in half diagonally to give four triangles.

Ⓒ Two 4½ x 2½in (11.2 x 6.2cm) strips.

Construction

Half-square Triangles, see 27

Four-patch, see 13

188 Floating Diamond

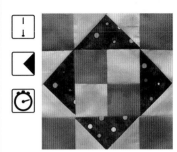

Cut the following

Ⓐ Six 2in (5cm) squares.

Ⓑ Ten 2in (5cm) squares.

Ⓒ Four 3½ x 2in (8.7 x 5cm) strips.

Construction

Fast Geese, see 134

Four-patch, see 13

Nine-patch, see 51

Mix and match

 108 147 169

Mix and match

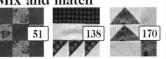 51 138 170

Mix and match

 33 100 173

189 Friendship Name Chain

Cut the following

 A B C D E

(A) One piece using template 189a.

(B) One 3⅛in (7.7cm) square cut in half diagonally to give two triangles; you need one of them.

(C) One 3⅛in (7.7cm) square cut in half diagonally to give two triangles; you need one of them.

(D) Two 3⅛in (7.7cm) squares cut in half diagonally to give four triangles; you need three of them.

(E) Two 3⅛in (7.7cm) squares cut in half diagonally to give four triangles; you need three of them.

Construction

 Bird in the Air, see 110

Fold the template piece in half and mark the centre with a crease. Sew a pieced unit to each side of the template piece, aligning the centre points with the crease.

---

190 Aircraft

Cut the following

 A B

(A) Five 2⅜in (5.8cm) squares cut in half diagonally to give ten triangles; you need nine of them.

(A) One 3⅞in (9.5cm) square cut in half diagonally to give two triangles; you need one of them.

(B) Two 2⅜in (5.8cm) squares cut in half diagonally to give four triangles; you need three of them.

(B) Two 3⅞in (9.5cm) squares cut in half diagonally to give four triangles.

Construction

Half-square Triangles, see 27
Bird in the Air, see 110
Four-patch, see 13

---

191 Checked Corner

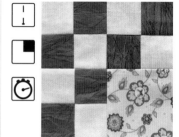

Cut the following

(A) (B) (A)

(A) Six 2in (5cm) squares.
(B) Six 2in (5cm) squares.
(C) One 3½in (8.7cm) square.

Construction

Four-patch, see 13

Mix and match

 49 80 153

Mix and match

 28 140 192

Mix and match

 2 187 192

192 Strength in Union Variation

Cut the following

A Eight 2in (5cm) squares.
B Four 2⅜in (5.8cm) squares cut in half diagonally to give eight triangles.
C Four 2⅜in (5.8cm) squares cut in half diagonally to give eight triangles.

Construction

Half-square Triangles, see 27
Four-patch, see 13

193 Even Stripes

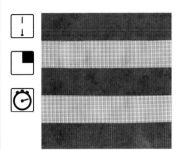

Cut the following

A Three 6½ x 1¾in (16.2 x 4.2cm) strips.
B Two 6½ x 1¾in (16.2 x 4.2cm) strips.

Construction

Stripes, see 99

194 Christmas Tree

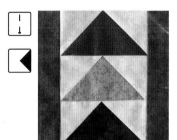

Cut the following

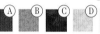

A One 4½ x 2½in (11.2 x 6.2cm) strip.
B One 4½ x 2½in (11.2 x 6.2cm) strip.
C One 4½ x 2½in (11.2 x 6.2cm) strip.
D Six 2½in (6.2cm) squares.
E Two 6½ x 1½in (16.2 x 3.7cm) strips.

Construction

Fast Geese, see 134
Stripes, see 99

Mix and match

23 123 140

20 194 199

137 141 175

CONSTRUCTION GUIDELINES

195 Courthouse Steps

Cut the following

(A) One 2in (5cm) square.

(B) Two 2 x 1¼in
(5 x 3.1cm) strips.

(C) Two 3½ x 1¼in
(8.7 x 3.1cm) strips.

(D) Two 3½ x 1¼in
(8.7 x 3.1cm) strips.

(E) Two 5 x 1¼in
(12.4 x 3.1cm) strips.

(F) Two 5 x 1¼in
(12.4 x 3.1cm) strips.

(G) Two 6½ x 1¼in
(16.2 x 3.1cm) strips.

Continue adding
matching strips
to opposite sides
of the block
until complete.

Quick tip

Instead of cutting the strips to
length before piecing, add them
to the block and trim them level
with the edges each time. Make
sure you keep the edges square.

Construction

Sew the shortest
strips to opposite
sides of the centre square.

Add the next two
strips on the
opposite sides.

Mix and match

 63
 102
 159

196 Sashed Triangles

Cut the following

 A B C D

(A) Four 1½in (3.7cm) squares.

(B) Four 4½ x 1½in
(11.2 x 3.7cm) strips.

(C) Two 2⅞in (7.2cm) squares
cut in half diagonally to give
four triangles.

(D) Two 2⅞in (7.2cm) squares
cut in half diagonally to give
four triangles.

Construction

Half-square Triangles, see 27

Four-patch, see 13

Nine-patch, see 51

Mix and match

 100
 173
 175

197 Grandmother's Corner

Cut the following

A B C

(A) One 2½in (6.2cm) square.

(A) One 4⅞in (12cm) square cut
in half diagonally to give two
triangles; you need one of them.

(B) Two 4½ x 2½in
(11.2 x 6.2cm) strips.

(C) One 4⅞in (12cm) square cut
in half diagonally to give two
triangles; you need one of them.

Construction

Half-square Triangles, see 27

Four-patch, see 13

Mix and match

 116
138
 166

198 Corner in the Cabin

Cut the following

(A) One 2in (5cm) square.

(B) One 3½ x 2in
(8.7 x 5cm) strip.

(C) One 5 x 2in
(12.4 x 5cm) strip.

(D) One 6½ x 2in
(16.2 x 5cm) strip.

(E) One 2in (5cm) square.

(F) One 3½ x 2in
(8.7 x 5cm) strip.

(G) One 5 x 2in
(12.4 x 5cm) strip.

Add the shortest dark-coloured strip.

Sew the next light- and dark-coloured strips in place in the same way, making sure that you maintain the light/dark balance.

Add the final light-coloured strip.

Construction

Sew the two squares together.

Add the shortest light-coloured strip.

---

199 Sixteen Squares

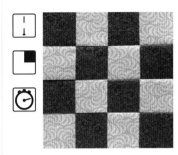

Cut the following

(A) Eight 2in (5cm) squares.

(B) Eight 2in (5cm) squares.

Construction

Four-patch, see 13

Mix and match

83   112   199

---

200 Geese Around the Corner

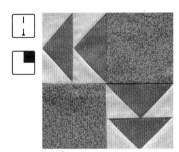

Cut the following

(A) Two 3½in (8.7cm) squares.

(B) Four 3½ x 2in
(8.7 x 5cm) strips.

(C) Eight 2in (5cm) squares.

Construction

Fast Geese, see 134

Four-patch, see 13

Mix and match

75   154   190

Techniques
and Templates

In this chapter you will find a summary of the techniques needed to piece and join the blocks in the directory. There are also suggestions on what equipment and threads to use, as well as ideas for binding and quilting your finished piece. Templates are provided for any curved pieces and difficult shapes required to make the blocks.

Equipment

All you need to start making the blocks in this book are a few sewing tools. The basic essentials are scissors, needle, fabric and thread. However, there are other tools that have been designed to make quilters' lives easier.

Scissors

Sharp fabric scissors for cutting fabrics (if you are not using a rotary cutter) and a small pair of scissors for cutting threads are best. Keep a separate pair for cutting paper and cardboard or plastic for templates.

Pins

Dressmaking pins are fine to use for quilting. Flat-headed (or flower-headed) pins are useful for machine sewing because the flat head does not catch under the foot if you sew over the pin by mistake. Thin appliqué pins are good for sewing curves, where you need to match the seams accurately.

Needles for hand sewing

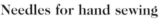

Buy a mixed packet to find the most comfortable size for you. Longer needles are useful when tacking the layers of a quilt together, and 'betweens' (special quilting needles) can be used for hand quilting.

Safety pins

These can be used to hold the layers of a quilt together ready for quilting, and are most useful if you are machine quilting because tacking threads can get caught on the foot of the machine as you sew.

Needles for machine sewing

Quilting needles have the sharpest point, but a universal needle in size 70 or 80 (European) – 10 or 12 (US) – can also be used. Always start a new project with a new needle; it is a small expense.

Thread

For piecing, use cotton sewing thread if you are using cotton fabrics. Some quilters use a taupe or sand colour whatever the colour of the fabric, but if your quilt is all blues, for example, you could use blue thread. The thread should not be visible on the finished quilt top. Quilting thread is used for hand or machine quilting and is heavier than standard sewing thread. It is available in variegated as well as plain colours. Decorative threads are also available.

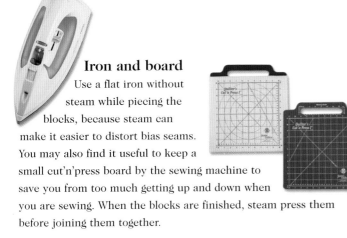

Iron and board

Use a flat iron without steam while piecing the blocks, because steam can make it easier to distort bias seams. You may also find it useful to keep a small cut'n'press board by the sewing machine to save you from too much getting up and down when you are sewing. When the blocks are finished, steam press them before joining them together.

Ruler

As the blocks in this book are small, you only need small rulers. A 4 x 14in ruler is ideal for cutting strips because it is long enough to cut through a fat quarter when folded and wide enough for most of the pieces used in the blocks. Other sizes, such as small squares – 2½in, 3½in and so on – are useful for trimming units to size, plus a 6½in square for checking the finished blocks. If you have a choice of rulers, choose one with 45- and 60-degree markings for cutting angled pieces. Look also at the lines on the ruler; many are marked on both sides, one dark and one light, which is useful for reading the measurements on different coloured fabrics. There are also turnaround rulers that give inches in bold on one side and ⅛in measurements in bold on the reverse. Metric versions of many sizes are also available.

Rotary cutter

Rotary cutters come in all shapes and sizes. Try to find one in the shop that is not in a packet so that you can hold it and see what it feels like in your hand; some may be more comfortable than others. If you have small children, choose one with a lock so that it cannot be accidentally used.

Self-healing cutting mat

Buy the largest mat you have room for. If you have to move your fabric to finish a cut, there is a chance that you will not cut straight. Only use a rotary cutter on a self-healing mat, not on another surface, because the cutter will damage the surface and the blade.

Sewing machine

A simple machine that does straight stitch is all that is necessary, but a needle-down function is useful for some of the inset seams and curved pieces because it enables you to work more slowly and stop to adjust the fabric. If you will be quilting by machine, look for plenty of space between the needle and the body of the machine, because this is where you will have the quilt gathered up as you stitch – the more room there is, the better.

Turntable

A turntable is useful if you are cutting large pieces and trimming them to size, because you can just spin the turntable around to cut each side without having to pick up and move the pieces. This helps to improve accuracy.

Wadding

Also known as batting, this is the padded layer between the quilt top and backing fabric. It can be purchased by the yard or metre, or in pre-cut sizes such as twin bed or crib size. Beginners may find it easier to work with thinner wadding. Thick polyester wadding can be used for making tied quilts, giving them a puffier appearance.

Cutting Fabrics

Y ou can cut the pieces of fabric for your blocks using scissors, but rotary cutting is a lot quicker and easier. Rotary cutters can be used to cut through two or more layers of fabric at one time. Left-handed people may find it easier to hold this book to a mirror to see the hand positions. See page 116 for cutting pieces using templates.

Strips

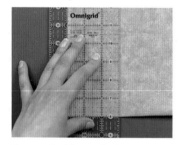

Position the fabric and ruler on the cutting mat.

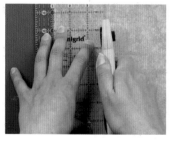

Guide the rotary cutter along the ruler to cut the fabric into strips.

1 Fold the fabric if needed so that it all fits on the cutting mat. Position one of the horizontal lines on the ruler along the fold, then position the vertical line marking the required width of the strips on the left-hand side of the fabric. Hold the ruler in place firmly and, if possible, have one finger off the ruler on the fabric or board. This helps to stabilize the ruler and you are less likely to push it out of position.

2 With the blade right against the ruler and off the edge of the fabric, start cutting away from you; never cut towards you for safety reasons.

Cut along one diagonal of a square to produce two half-square triangles.

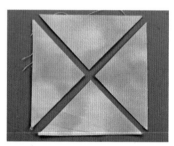

Cut along both diagonals to produce four quarter-square triangles.

Triangles

1 To cut a half-square triangle, cut squares of the required size and cut along one diagonal to produce two triangles.

2 For quarter-square triangles, cut the squares along both diagonals to give four small triangles.

Squares and rectangles

To cut strips into squares or rectangles, leave them folded. Position the fabric and align the ruler in the same way as before to cut across the fabric in the opposite direction. If you are using a turntable, you can simply spin the board around rather than reposition the fabric.

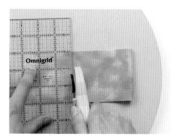

Using a turntable to cut strips into squares and rectangles saves time.

Angles

1 To cut strips of fabric at an angle (only 45-degree angles are required for the blocks in this book), align the 45-degree line on the ruler with the bottom edge of the fabric and cut as usual.

2 Some quilters find it helpful to make a paper template and attach it with transparent tape to the ruler to remind them of what the finished piece should look like. This avoids the common problem of trimming the wrong end, or the wrong angle. You can also buy small brightly coloured strips that temporarily attach to the ruler to do the same job.

Align the ruler at the required angle and cut diagonally.

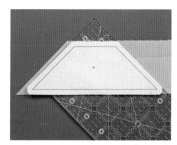

Attaching a paper template to the ruler may help you avoid making mistakes.

Fabric grain

Fabrics are made by weaving lengthways and crossways threads together. Fabric therefore has two straight grains, where these threads run parallel to or at right angles to the selvage (the finished edge). When cutting patches, orient them so that the straight grains will run vertically and horizontally through the blocks. The bias grain of the fabric – that is, the diagonal grain that runs at a 45-degree angle to the selvage – is more stretchy than the straight grains. When possible, avoid cutting pieces with seams on the bias grain, because it has a tendency to stretch and distort the blocks. However, many blocks and pieced units require bias seams (half-square triangles, for example) and these should be sewn slowly to avoid distorting the pieces. Blocks that include diamonds will have at least two sides on the bias grain. Avoid having bias edges on the outside edges of blocks because it makes the quilt harder to assemble well.

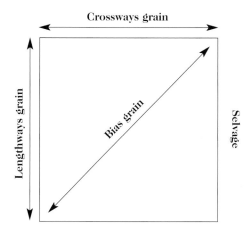

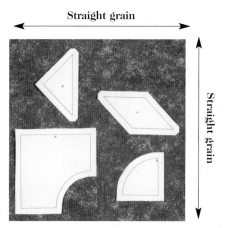

Piecing Techniques

Blocks can be sewn by hand or machine, but machine sewing is much faster. Use small, evenly spaced running stitches when sewing by hand; use a straight running stitch for machine sewing, setting the stitch length to between 9 and 12 stitches per inch (2.5cm).

Regular shapes

Lay out the pieces in the correct order.

1 Lay out the pieces in the correct positions and join them into rows. Start by placing the first two units right sides together and sew with a ¼in (6mm) seam allowance. Keep adding pieces until you have completed each row. Press the seams (see box).

2 Join the rows together, matching and pinning the seams if necessary, then press the finished block.

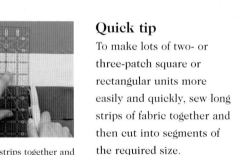

For speed, join strips together and then cut them to the required size.

Quick tip

To make lots of two- or three-patch square or rectangular units more easily and quickly, sew long strips of fabric together and then cut into segments of the required size.

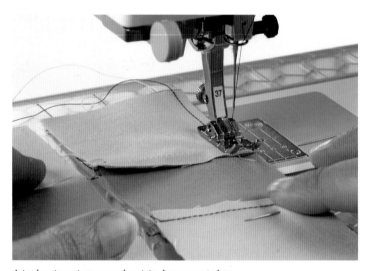

Join the pieces into rows, then join the rows together.

Chain piecing

Chain piecing is a way of sewing identical pieces quickly. Place the first pair under the machine foot and start sewing. When you reach the end of the seam, instead of lifting the presser foot, simply feed the next pair of pieces into the space and continue sewing. You will sew across a small gap and then the feed dogs will pick up the fabric of the new pieces. Cut the thread to separate the pieces when you have finished. Once you become proficient, you need hardly slow down at all. This method also saves a lot of thread.

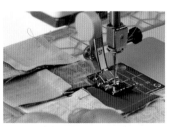

Feed pieces through the machine closely together and then cut the thread to separate them.

Inset seams

1 Inset seams have one piece that has to be stitched into an angle formed by other pieces; they cannot be sewn in a straight line. Mark the seam allowances at the corner points with a dot. Sew the first two pieces together, stopping at the dots (if you continue to the edges of the fabric, you will not be able to add the inset piece).

2 Clip the corner of the inset piece almost as far as the seam allowance; this will help you to pivot the pieces when sewing, and the fabric is more likely to pucker if the allowance is not clipped. Place the pieces right sides together with the inset section on top. Start at one edge and sew to the next dot. Leave the needle in the fabric, raise the presser foot and pivot the fabric so that the next two dots line up, then pin and complete the sewing.

Curved seams

1 Although some quilters clip the seam allowances when sewing curves, this can weaken the block and is unnecessary for the gentle curves required in this book. Mark the centre of both curves by folding and pinching a small crease at the edge of the fabric.

2 Pin together the outer edges, midpoint and regular intervals in between, with the concave section on top. Insert the pins at a right angle to the seam so that you can pull them out at the last moment when sewing; it is much harder to pin along the seam line on a curve. Starting at one edge, slowly sew the seam, pulling the top fabric into place as you go; use a smaller stitch than usual. Where there is more than one curve, start with the smallest and continue adding the remaining curved pieces until the block is complete.

Mark the seam allowances at each corner of the pieces with a dot.

Sew from dot to dot, pivoting the fabric around the needle when you are ready to sew the next seam.

Fold and crease the fabric to mark the centre points of the curved edges.

Pin the curved edges together, inserting the pins at right angles. When you sew the seam, the pins can be removed easily at the last moment.

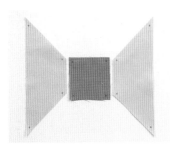

If using a pale fabric, press the seams towards the darker fabric where possible.

Pressing seams

When all the pieces are joined into rows, press the seam allowances on the first row to the right, on the second row to the left and so on down the block. If you press them all to the same side, you will get a bump of seam allowances on one side of the seam when you sew the rows together. Where blocks start with a central point, such as log cabin designs, it is best to press the seams away from the centre each time. For curved pieces, the fabric will lie flatter if you press the seams towards the outside of the block. If your fabric is very pale, you may want to press towards the darkest fabric.

Improving Accuracy

An accurate seam allowance is important because, if it is uneven, the units of the block will not meet up neatly and your blocks may be of uneven sizes. Here are a few ideas for improving your accuracy.

Seam allowances

Sew strips of equal width together, alternating the colours, and press the seam allowances in one direction.

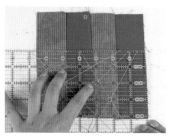

Measure the top, middle and bottom of the strips to check they are equal.

1 The first step to improving accuracy is to test your seam allowance. Cut four 6½ x 2in (16.2 x 5cm) strips of fabric from two or more different colours. Sew the strips together along the long edges, alternating the colours. Press all the seam allowances in one direction and lay the block on a cutting board.

2 With a square ruler, measure the width of all the strips. The outer two that have only lost one seam allowance should measure 1¾in (4.2cm), and the inner strips that have lost both seam allowances should measure 1½in (3.7cm). Next, check that the ends of the strips are as accurate as the middles. It is common to slope off at the beginning and end of a seam. One way of preventing this is to start and stop stitching on a small scrap of fabric and feed your material through, aligning it with the ¼in (6mm) foot of the machine.

Quick tip

If you do not have a ¼in (6mm) foot, mark the measurement on the bed of the sewing machine. Place the edge of a ruler precisely under the needle and stick some tape exactly ¼in (6mm) to the right. If you pile up three of four layers of tape, it will give a nice edge to work to.

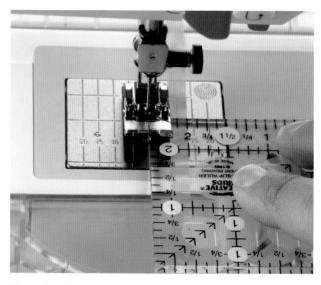

Use a ruler and tape to mark the bed of your sewing machine ¼in (6mm) to the right of the needle to indicate an accurate seam allowance.

Cut larger squares than required, sew together on either side of the diagonal, then cut along the diagonal, open out and trim to the correct size.

Do the same to make accurate quarter-square triangles, sewing on either side of both diagonals and then cutting and trimming to size.

Half- and quarter-square triangles

1 The most accurate method is to add ⅛in (3mm) to the cut size of squares specified. Place the squares right sides together, draw a diagonal line on the reverse of one of the fabrics and sew ¼in (6mm) either side of the line. Cut apart on the line and press open. Place the pieced squares on your cutting board and, using a small square ruler, trim to the required size. Place the 45-degree line on the ruler along the diagonal seam to ensure that you are trimming accurately to a square.

2 You can use the same method with quarter-square triangles, cutting the initial squares ⅛in (3mm) larger as before and then trimming the finished pieced squares.

Quick tip

It is worth comparing the markings on your rulers. There are several makes and some have wider markings than others. You might find that cutting to one side or other of the line makes your work more accurate.

Fast corners

1 Fast corners can be used for snowball blocks and flying geese units. For these, cut a square and place it right sides together on the required corner. Sew just one thread's width away from the diagonal in the direction of the corner.

2 Fold back and press the square towards the corner. The thread's width allowance means that it should exactly match the edges of the corner. Cut away the excess fabric from the back.

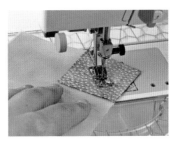

Sew a square to the required corner, a thread's width closer to the corner than the diagonal.

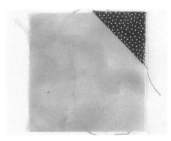

Fold back the square and press towards the corner, then trim the excess fabric from the back.

Templates

When working with templates, you may find it reassuring to allow a ½in (12mm) seam allowance on the edge of the block and then trim to fit after the block is complete. Do not use this safety margin to allow sloppy piecing; you are still aiming for accuracy. After a while, you will not feel the need for this extra allowance; you will be able to piece perfectly all the time.

Unpicking

Unless it is unavoidable, do not unpick blocks. If you have made a mistake, cut new pieces and put the mistake onto your spare pieces pile. If you unpick the seam, you weaken and distort the fabrics. If you have sewn a whole block together wrongly, it might be a new variation – that could well be how many original blocks were developed.

Completing the Quilt

Piecing the finished blocks together is no more complicated than piecing a basic nine-patch block. The only difference is that the pieces are slightly larger and you may have a few more of them. The quilt top then needs to be sandwiched with wadding and backing fabric, and the layers quilted together.

Pin the blocks together.

Joining the blocks

If you have a complicated arrangement, pin the blocks in position onto a backing sheet. Check the arrangement carefully; it is better to discover now that a block needs rotating than after the quilt top is pieced together. A Polaroid or digital photo may also help you to analyze the arrangement. When you are satisfied, unpin the blocks from the backing sheet. Pin and then sew them into rows, pressing the seam allowances in alternate directions on each row and then join the rows together until you have one piece.

Sew the blocks together in rows, then join the rows to complete the quilt top.

Tacked layers.

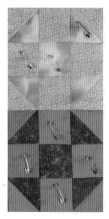

Pinned layers.

Preparing the layers

Join together sufficient fabric to make a piece of backing, allowing 2in (5cm) larger all around for a large quilt top or 1in (2.5cm) for a small quilt top or cushion. Press the quilt top and remove stray threads. Lay the backing right side down onto a flat, clean surface. Spread the wadding on top, smoothing it by hand to remove creases if necessary. Float the quilt top right side up onto the wadding. Starting from the centre, pin the three layers together. Use dressmaking pins if you will be tacking and hand quilting the quilt, but use safety pins if you will be machine quilting it. Place the pins or tacking stitches close enough together so that you cannot place your hand on the quilt without touching a pin or stitch.

Hand quilting

This is commonly a running stitch but can be backstitch or a decorative stitch, such as French knots or chain stitch. Begin quilting in the centre and work outwards; that way you can smooth creases towards the edges of the quilt top if necessary. Start by stitching through all three layers, pulling the knot at the end of the thread into the wadding layer. Continue sewing the design of your choice, using a rocking motion to collect two or more stitches onto the needle at once. Use a thimble to push the needle through the layers. Working in a hoop suits some people; try it and see. Remove the quilt from the hoop to avoid leaving permanent creases whenever you stop for a break (even if you only think you will be five minutes).

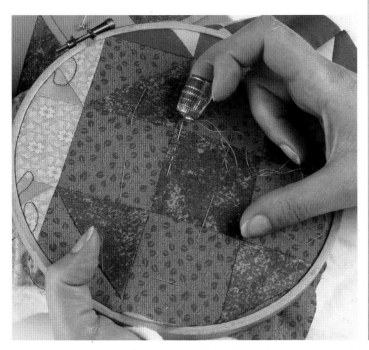

Use a rocking motion to collect two or more stitches onto the needle at once.

Machine quilting

Use seam lines as a guide for sewing straight lines of machine quilting.

Lower the feed dogs and use your hands to guide the quilt beneath the needle in the required design.

1 There are two styles of machine quilting. The first is with the feed dogs up and a foot on the machine that can be used to quilt in straight or slightly curved lines. For beginners, quilting a line parallel to but not in the seam line is easiest because you can put your machine foot against the seam and follow this as a guide. As with hand quilting, always start in the centre and work outwards.

2 The second method is free-motion quilting, with the feed dogs down and letting your hands guide the quilt to produce the pattern.

Tie the layers together with decorative knots instead of sewing them.

Quick tip

For a real utility quilt, just tie the three layers together with thread at intervals; the knots can be a decorative feature on the front or the back.

Templates

Several blocks in this book require pieces that are difficult to cut using standard measurements, so full-size drawings are provided here so that you can make templates. Note that these drawings **do not** include a ¼in (6mm) seam allowance.

Making templates

You can make templates with or without a seam allowance added. To make templates without a seam allowance, trace the required shapes onto greaseproof paper and glue them onto cardboard. If you have template plastic, you can draw directly onto this, tracing from the page. Cut out exactly on the line with scissors or a sharp craft knife. Use the same process to make templates that include a seam allowance, but add the seam allowance to the drawings in this book before tracing them. Photocopy the drawings if you do not wish to mark the book.

Cutting fabric

Place the templates onto the wrong side of the fabric and draw around them with short, stroking lines. Trying not to drag the fabric, continue off the end of any points to give sharp, accurate points. Remember to add a seam allowance if you have not already added it to the templates. Cut out with a rotary cutter or scissors.

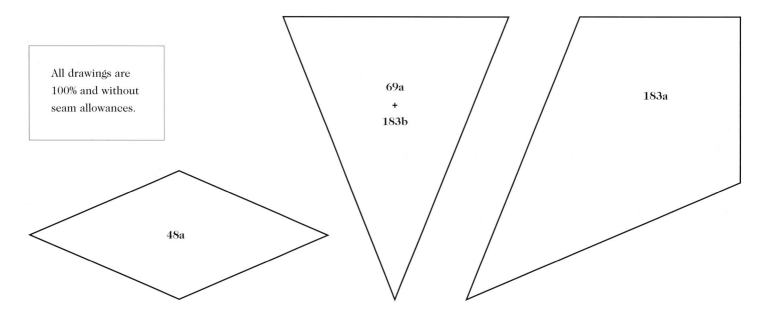

All drawings are 100% and without seam allowances.

48a

69a
+
183b

183a

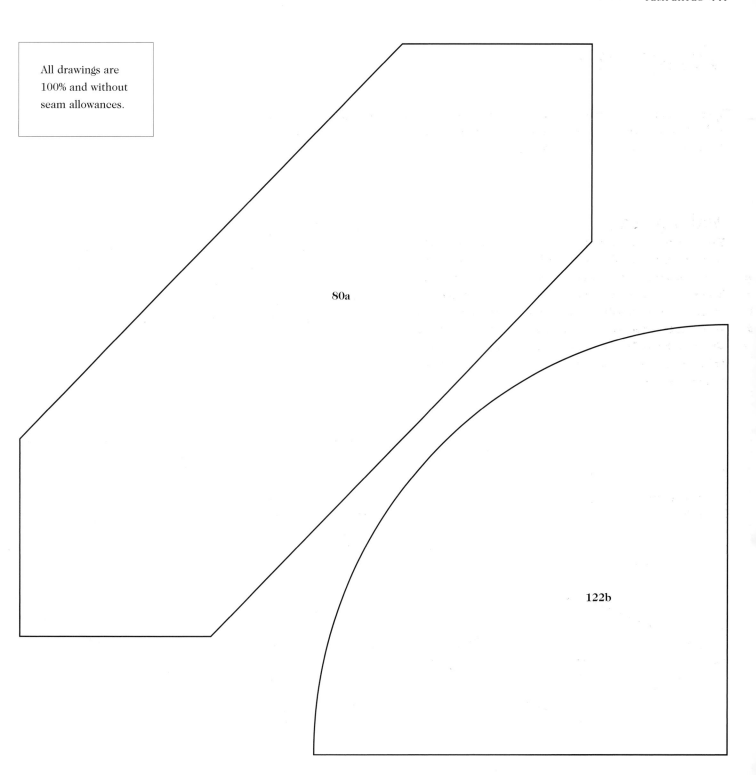

All drawings are
100% and without
seam allowances.

80a

122b

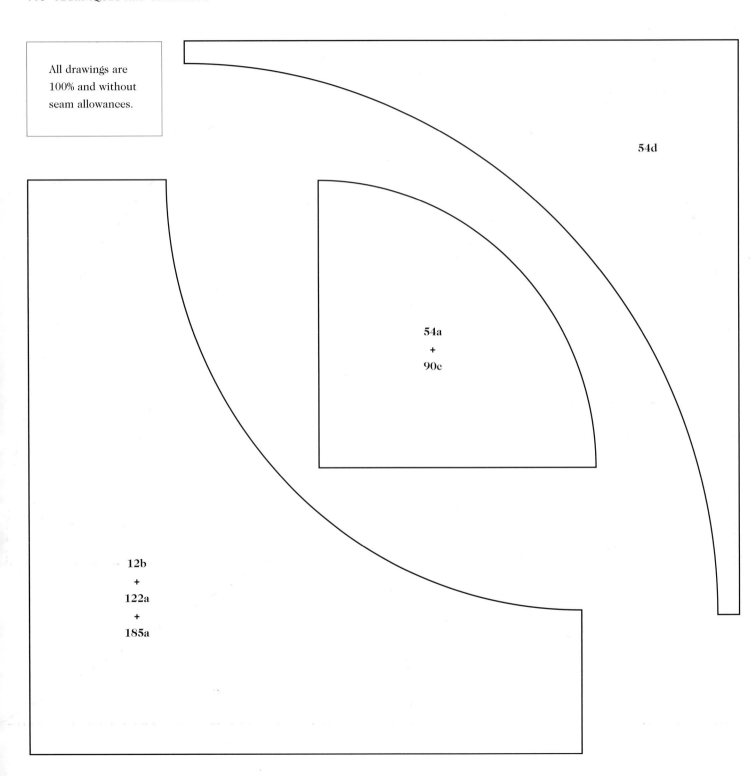

All drawings are
100% and without
seam allowances.

54d

54a
+
90c

12b
+
122a
+
185a

All drawings are
100% and without
seam allowances.

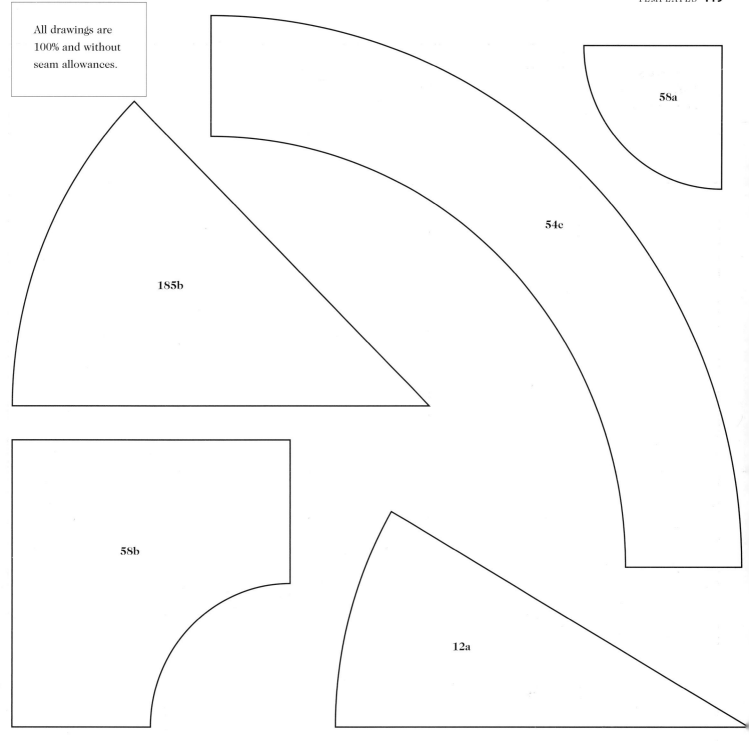

58a

54c

185b

58b

12a

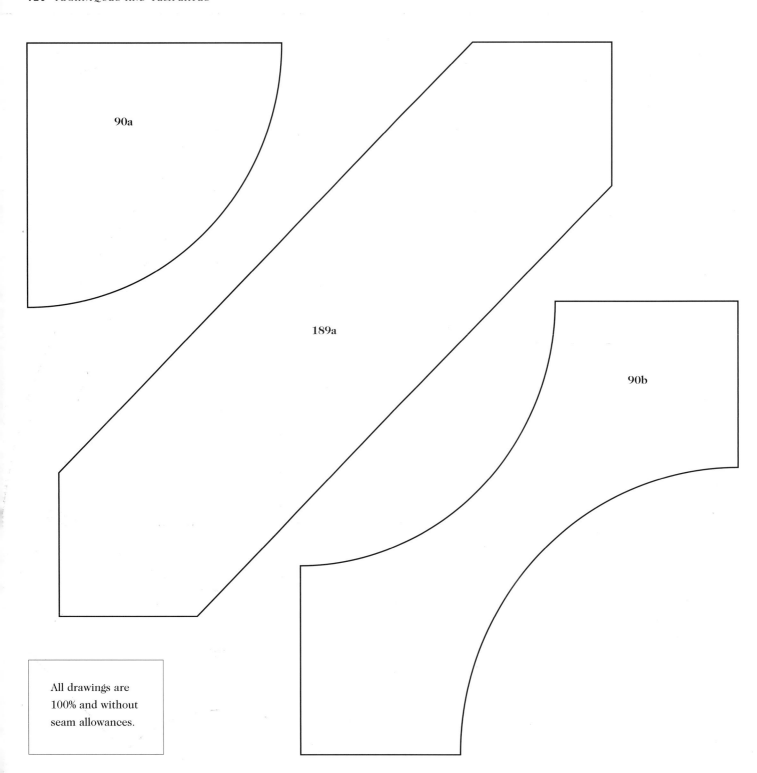

90a

189a

90b

All drawings are
100% and without
seam allowances.

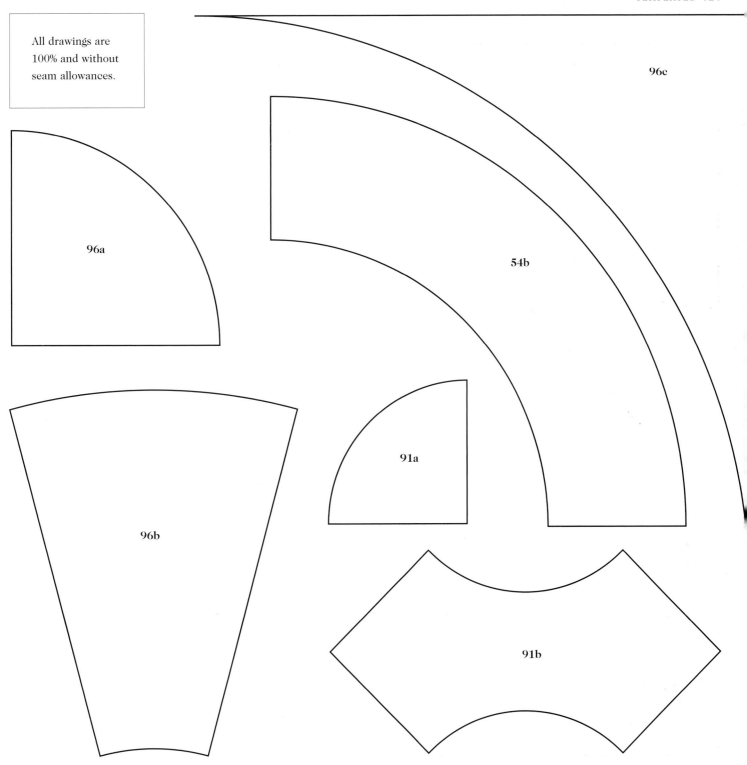

All drawings are
100% and without
seam allowances.

96a

96c

54b

96b

91a

91b

Fabric Resource Directory

When creating the blocks in this book, colours and patterns were chosen from a palette of 100 fabrics. Here is a list of the actual fabrics used, specifying the manufacturer's name, details of the fabric range and manufacturer's codes, plus the reference number of the blocks that feature the fabric. All the fabrics are 100 per cent cotton. Refer to page 128 for a selection of fabric suppliers.

 White: Bryan Taphouse, Nature's Moods, White 1 (blocks 31, 82, 131, 159)

 White swirls: Makower, White on White Pattern (blocks 33, 37, 136, 159, 165, 177)

 White with grey mist: Classic Cottons, S3171, P5751, C81T (blocks 75, 97, 105, 159, 166, 194, 196)

Green shells: Classic Cottons, S3296, P5461, C470T (blocks 47, 110, 133, 199)

Light green: Bryan Taphouse, Nature's Moods, Melon 37 (blocks 19, 22, 68, 78, 102, 121, 157)

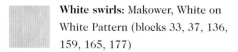 **Floral green:** Rowan, Gazania Leafy, G03LF (blocks 9, 19, 70, 78, 102, 121, 128, 180)

Hazy lime: Woodrow Studios, Colourplay, Lime Green (blocks 42, 59, 78, 141, 158, 162, 182)

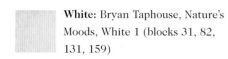 **Green gingham:** Michael Miller Fabrics, Crib Check, Green, C886 (blocks 7, 68, 115, 120, 163, 193)

 Tropical lime: Bryan Taphouse, Nature's Moods, Tropical Lime 49 (blocks 1, 55, 64, 75, 80, 82, 87, 124)

 Green sprigs: Classic Cottons, S3171, P5594, C64T (blocks 35, 47, 78, 113, 126, 189, 194)

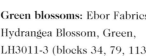 **Green blossoms:** Ebor Fabrics, Hydrangea Blossom, Green, LH3011-3 (blocks 34, 79, 113, 158, 189)

 Marbled green: Michael Miller Fabrics, Krystal, Dark Green (blocks 34, 153, 163, 180, 194)

Geometric blues: Makower, Vienna Triangles (blocks 114, 117, 137, 157)

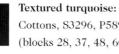 **Textured turquoise:** Classic Cottons, S3296, P5892, C52 (blocks 28, 37, 48, 60, 97, 116, 159, 165, 180)

 Turquoise triangles: Classic Cottons, S3416, P7082, C5 (blocks 57, 60, 76, 96, 117, 125, 134, 153)

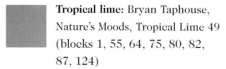 **Turquoise vines:** Michael Miller Fabrics, Vine Hearts, Turquoise, C1190 (blocks 4, 42, 54, 59, 109, 111, 187, 192)

Blue flower patch: Makower, Siam, 413 BT (blocks 10, 21, 30, 116, 156, 186)

 **Floral blue:** Makower, Siam, Floral Trail, 409 BT (blocks 32, 54, 89, 118, 143, 186, 191)

Sky blue with lightning streaks: Perfect Occasions, Summer Sky, 1003269 (blocks 48, 69, 139)

Hazy blue: Woodrow Studios, Colourplay, Turquoise (blocks 23, 50, 54, 59, 118, 125, 156)

Light blue spray: Makower, Spraytime, 2800 T32 (blocks 8, 42, 60, 114, 116, 134, 145, 150, 180, 191, 195)

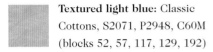 **Textured light blue:** Classic Cottons, S2071, P2948, C60M (blocks 52, 57, 117, 129, 192)

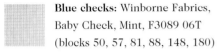 **Blue checks:** Winborne Fabrics, Baby Check, Mint, F3089 06T (blocks 50, 57, 81, 88, 148, 180)

Blue forget-me-nots: Classic Cottons, S3171, P5420, C22T (blocks 41, 97, 105, 140, 151, 180)

Powder blue: Bryan Taphouse, Nature's Moods, Turquoise 34 (blocks 30, 38, 57, 60, 77, 89, 103, 104, 114, 164)

Blue pansies: Classic Cottons, S3296, P5387, C29T (blocks 28, 57, 96, 150, 153, 165, 180)

Blue vines: Fabri-Quilt, Inc., Earth Wind and Fire (blocks 97, 107, 137, 151)

Misty blue: Erlanger, Better Than Basics (blocks 109, 111, 148, 165, 187)

Starry night blue: Moda Fabrics, Rainbow Stars, Blue (blocks 21, 42, 50, 54, 109, 174, 192)

Dark blue spray: Makower, Spraytime, 2800 B05 (blocks 2, 57, 111, 136, 159)

 Dark blue: Bryan Taphouse, Nature's Moods, Blue 67 (blocks 42, 51, 59, 75, 82, 87, 150)

 Psychedelic blue: Woodrow Studios, Millefiori Paperweights (blocks 23, 83, 112, 150, 156, 162)

 Indigo spray: Makower, Spraytime, 2800 B08 (blocks 21, 50, 69, 107, 116, 139, 151, 186)

 Textured dark blue: Classic Cottons, S2071, P2948, C23D (blocks 57, 60, 96, 104, 114, 129, 187, 191, 195)

 Blue and gold pansies: Makower, Pansy (blocks 2, 30, 52, 74, 96, 99, 145)

 Gold swirls on brown: Makower, Deco Oval Swirl (blocks 6, 67, 100, 180, 197)

 Textured brown: Classic Cottons, S3296, P5892, C42 (blocks 6, 20, 84, 173, 184)

 Brown vines: Classic Cottons, S3294, P5550, C96T (blocks 68, 86, 108, 123, 127, 142, 154)

 Gold speckle: Moda Fabrics, Thimbleberries, Quilt Club Collection, Gold Speckle, F5003-1 (blocks 66, 70, 100, 152, 200)

 Gold flowers: Moda Fabrics, Flower on Gold, 17033 12 (blocks 73, 84, 92, 123, 154, 170)

 Checkered gold: Benartex, Happy Holiday, Sleigh Crossings, Gold, S380, C30 (blocks 49, 72, 79, 169)

 Starry gold: Moda Fabrics, Bittersweet and Boo, Stars on Gold, 17032 12 (blocks 20, 67, 93, 99, 154, 189, 190, 197)

 Golden curls: Classic Cottons, S3296, P5963, C44 (blocks 9, 58, 119, 130, 183, 200)

 Berries on gold: Moda Fabrics, Thimbleberries, Berry Patch, 4866 C7 (blocks 7, 51, 68, 108, 173, 184, 189)

 Gold with holly: Benartex, Happy Holiday, Jolly Holly, Soft Gold, S381, C33 (blocks 49, 79, 175, 189)

 Yellow rose swag: Moda Fabrics, Gingham Rose, 3 Sisters, Yellow Stripe, F3703-14 (blocks 3, 35, 86, 126, 130)

 Golden roses: Anbo Textiles, Tudor Garden, Rose Gold, F173-190 (blocks 2, 61, 93, 108, 142, 152)

Cream zigzags: Moda Fabrics, Colombia River, 7966 11 (blocks 53, 73, 85, 126, 127)

 Cream flower patch: Makower, Two-Tone Petal, Cream, 0304 (blocks 34, 100, 170, 183, 197)

 Patterned cream: Timeless Treasures, Ivory Noel, F5426, C2426 (blocks 26, 30, 44, 67, 84, 170, 195, 200)

 Vanilla spatter: Michael Miller Fabrics, Countertop Texture, Vanilla, C239 (blocks 6, 27, 66, 96, 138, 155, 195)

 Lemon: Bryan Taphouse, Nature's Moods, Lemon 38 (blocks 3, 20, 58, 70, 90, 123, 154, 167)

 Lemon stripes: Anbo Textiles, Fine Lemon Stripes, S3000, C503 (blocks 13, 45, 173)

 Banana yellow: Bryan Taphouse, Nature's Moods, Banana Yellow 40 (blocks 77, 80, 82, 144, 168)

 Yellow spray: Makower, Spraytime, 2800 Y08 (blocks 29, 75, 78, 83, 147, 160, 168)

 Gold spray: Makower, Spraytime, 2800 N06 (blocks 16, 62, 92, 108, 160, 162, 168)

 Gold leaves: Classic Cottons, S3281, P6383, C45T (blocks 12, 17, 39, 98, 147, 169, 177)

 Orange sprigs: Classic Cottons, S3281, P4388, C72T (blocks 65, 91, 105, 169, 172)

 Orange leaves: Classic Cottons, S3281, P6384, C74T (blocks 12, 17, 62, 75, 105, 121, 172)

 Bright orange: Bryan Taphouse, Nature's Moods, Orange 41 (blocks 5, 87, 147, 160, 168, 178)

 Red gingham: Michael Miller Fabrics, Crib Check, Red, C886 (blocks 33, 94, 95, 115, 159, 179)

 Pink sprigs: Classic Cottons, S3171, P5594, C14T (blocks 11, 76, 94, 101, 105)

 Apricot: Bryan Taphouse, Nature's Moods, Apricot 23 (blocks 43, 81, 94, 132, 133, 146, 164)

 Psychedelic orange: Rowan, FG01RD 0304450 (blocks 12, 18, 39, 64, 87, 128, 131, 176, 178)

 Dotted red: Michael Miller Fabrics, Pindot, Red, C1065 (blocks 37, 45, 55, 115, 160)

 Red leaves: Classic Cottons, S3296, P5589, C13T (blocks 4, 47, 94, 105, 106, 158, 162)

 Red flower patch: Classic Cottons, S3171, P5466, C76T (blocks 16, 22, 65, 78, 91, 95, 105, 179)

 Bright red: Bryan Taphouse, Nature's Moods, Christmas Red 44 (blocks 31, 40, 82, 90, 112, 167)

 Red spray: Makower, Spraytime, 2800 R04 (blocks 17, 29, 33, 62, 83, 161, 193, 194)

 Marbled red: Moda Fabrics, Marbles, Turkey Red, F6854 (blocks 3, 49, 78, 94, 105, 120, 126, 169)

 Abstract orange: Makower, Verona Abstract (blocks 27, 93, 135, 175, 190)

 Marbled ginger: Moda Fabrics, Ginger Marble, F7521-16 (blocks 6, 53, 61, 74, 108, 119, 130, 154)

 Ginger checks: Moda Fabrics, Bittersweet and Boo, Ginger Check, 17031 16 (blocks 13, 73, 92, 138, 180)

 Blue and cream diamonds: Makower, Nile Mosaic, 3804 (blocks 44, 67, 85, 138, 155, 195)

 Grey mosaic with stars: Moda Fabrics, Thimbleberries, Star Grid, F5018-3 (blocks 40, 90, 167, 184, 198)

Grey leaves: Classic Cottons, S3281, P6384, C84T (blocks 140, 159, 166, 198)

 Blue-grey checkers: Moda Fabrics, Thimbleberries, Berry Patch, Blue Diamonds, F4865 (blocks 4, 41, 88, 125, 153, 166, 195, 198)

 Green flower patch: Classic Cottons, S3171, P5466, C67T (blocks 26, 35, 70, 72, 175, 194, 199)

 Black: Bryan Taphouse, Nature's Moods, Black 81 (blocks 18, 31, 98, 135, 164)

 Multicoloured scissors on black: Michael Miller Fabrics, Scizzors, Black, C2214 (blocks 5, 36, 39, 144, 164, 168)

 Grape: Bryan Taphouse, Nature's Moods, Grape 62 (blocks 38, 78, 131, 147, 153, 178)

 Violet vines: Classic Cottons, S3296, P5550, C31T (blocks 15, 46, 109, 129, 147, 186, 196)

 Multicoloured spots on purple: Moda Fabrics, Multi Dot, Purple, F9913-13 (blocks 12, 24, 39, 117, 128, 171, 181, 188)

 Hazy purple: Woodrow Studios, Colourplay, Purple (blocks 8, 78, 102, 113, 147, 156, 171, 176, 188)

 Violet splash: Timeless Treasures, Atlas Multi, F3148, C3148 (blocks 28, 46, 56, 113, 156, 186)

 Purple circles: Michael Miller Fabrics, Disco Dot, Violet, C910 (blocks 38, 149)

 Hazy lilac: Woodrow Studios, Colourplay, Lilac (blocks 71, 118, 122, 149, 171, 196)

 Lilac: Bryan Taphouse, Nature's Moods, Lilac 29 (blocks 18, 56, 60, 132, 153, 156)

 Floral pastels: Ebor Fabrics, Hydrangea and Raspberry, LH3007110 (blocks 34, 113, 122, 198)

 Pink leaves on cream: Classic Cottons, S3281, P6387, C10T (blocks 15, 16, 25, 65, 103, 105, 106, 113)

 Rosebuds on cream: Moda Fabrics, Peach Roses on Cream (blocks 47, 103, 146, 185, 198)

 Flower sprinkle on cream: Anbo Textiles, Pink Flower Sprinkle, F6100-10 (blocks 43, 76, 133, 153, 198)

 Roses on pink: Moda Fabrics, Paris Flea Market, Pink Ribbon Roses, F3726-16 (blocks 11, 110, 158, 161, 198)

 Baby pink: Bryan Taphouse, Nature's Moods, Ice Pink 27 (blocks 14, 24, 47, 63, 81, 94, 185)

 Hazy pink: Woodrow Studios, Colourplay, Pink (blocks 15, 46, 56, 71, 118, 128, 143, 171, 185, 188)

 Tropical pink with butterflies: Michael Miller Fabrics, Tropical Fizz, Pink, C2208 (blocks 1, 10, 63, 64, 124, 182)

 Marbled pink: Michael Miller Fabrics, Krystal, Pink (blocks 25, 32, 39, 131, 141, 147, 171, 181, 196)

 Wide pastel stripes: Michael Miller Fabrics, Colorband, Pastel, C1257 (blocks 14, 36, 81, 101, 103, 132, 164, 171)

 Thin pastel stripes: Michael Miller Fabrics, Pencil Stripe, Turquoise, C1003 (blocks 38, 104, 174, 195)

 Multicoloured mosaic: Michael Miller Fabrics, Quilt, Multi, C2215 (blocks 5, 55, 77, 82, 168)

Index

Stockists and Manufacturers

Fabrics

Anbo Textiles
www.anbo.co.uk

Benartex
www.benartex.com

Classic Cottons
www.classiccottons.com

Ebor Fabrics
www.egnet.co.uk

Erlanger
www.clothpeddlar.com
www.quiltknit.com

Fabri-Quilt, Inc.
www.fabri-quilt.com

Makower
www.andoverfabrics.com
www.makoweruk.com

Michael Miller Fabrics
www.michaelmillerfabrics.com

Moda Fabrics/United Notions
www.modafabrics.com

Perfect Occasions
& Bryan Tapho
www.bombaystoresonline.com
www.cottonpatch.co.uk

Rowan
www.coatscraft.co.uk
www.knitrowan.com

Winbourne Fabrics Limited
www.winbofabrics.co.uk

Quilting supplies

Barossa Quilt & Craft Cottage
www.barossaquilt.com.au

Becky Sharp's Quilting
www.becky-sharps-quilting.com

The Cloth Shop
www.clothshop.co.uz

Creations Direct
www.creationsdirect.co.uk

Creative Grids Ltd
www.creativegrids.com

Creative Quilting
www.creativequilting.co.uk

Dreamcatcher Quilts
www.dreamcatcherquilts.co.uk

Exquisite Stitch
www.exquisitestitch.co.nz

Fun 2 Do
www.fun2do.co.uk

Honeysuckle Cottage
www.honeysucklecottage.
   com.au

House of Patchwork
www.houseofpatchwork.co.uk

Needlecraft
www.needecraft.co.nz

Patchwork by Sea
www.patchworkbysea.com.au

Patchwork Direct
www.patchworkdirect.com

The Patchwork Gallery
www.home.btclick.com/
   patchworkgallery

Patchwork Plus
www.patchworkplus.co.uk

Pauline's Patchwork
www.paulinespatchwork.co.uk

The Quilters Cabin
www.thequilterscabin.co.nz

The Quilt Room
www.quiltroom.co.uk

Rio Designs
www.riodesigns.co.uk

Stitchin' Stuff
www.stitchingstuff.co.nz

Stitch in Time
www.stitchintime.co.uk

Strawberry Fayre
www.strawberryfayre.co.uk

Credits

All photographs and illustrations are the copyright of Quarto Publishing plc.

While every effort has been made to credit contributors, Quarto would like to apologize should there have been any omissions or errors, and would be pleased to make the appropriate correction for future editions of the book.